Spirituality Made Simple

This book makes universal spiritual laws of awareness and purpose available in the simplest language possible in the form of a dialogue between Suraj and Cathy. It makes cosmic principles easy to understand and practise in our daily lives.

The importance of relationships in our spiritual growth is emphasised. The author has explained how two people can accept each other and thereby become more fulfilled, happy and complete individuals.

Happiness must not be a mere concept which should only be discussed and debated, but a true value which should be apparent in our lives and must pervade our interactions with people.

Vikas Malkani has been involved in spirituality from a young age, and has been fortunate enough to have met and learnt from many spiritual masters. He counsels people on emotional and spiritual problems, and guides them to become more complete and fulfilled human beings. His articles on spiritual living have been published by various magazines.

An inspirational speaker, Vikas gives talks on spiritual principles and their application to daily living. He was raised in a business family and has studied in India and the United States. Since the call became too strong to ignore, he has dedicated his time and energy to helping people in their self-development towards becoming more efficient and harmonious individuals.

He resides in New Delhi, but spends his time between India and the United States, helping people in both countries.

SPIRITUALITY
MADE
SIMPLE

Vikas Malkani

New Dawn

NEW DAWN
a division of Sterling Publishers (P) Ltd.
L-10, Green Park Extension, New Delhi-110016
Tel : 6191023, 6191784/85; Fax : 91-11-6190028
E-mail: ghai@nde.vsnl.net.in

Spirituality Made Simple
©1999, Vikas Malkani
ISBN 81 207 2165 9
First Edition 1997
Published under the title
The Grass is always Greener
Second Edition 1999
Reprint 2000

Published by Sterling Publishers Pvt. Ltd., New Delhi-110016.
Lasertypeset by Vikas Compographics, New Delhi-110029.
Printed at Shagun Offset. New Delhi-110020.
Cover design by Sterling Studio

To God,

who has always watched and guided me,
and has given me so much.
All that I am, and have,
is through Him.

"If God be for us,
who can be against us?"

Romans 8 : 31

CONTENTS

PREFACE

For many years, my friends and those I have helped had urged me to write a book and make it accessible to seekers worldwide — a book which would make available to them my views on life and my way of explaining the spiritual principles of this universe. For years, I ignored the message or didn't take the suggestions seriously.

Then, in the summer of 1997, when I was going through a period of tremendous inner growth and change, came a day when all kinds of blocks (mostly mental and spiritual) fell away and the message came across from my heart, extremely loud and extremely clear. It was more a command than a suggestion. This was what I was put here to do. And there was just no ignoring or denying it anymore.

Here then is the result of my walking the path. I pray that it shall make yours a little easier.

THE INITIAL MEETING

I remember I was 30 years old when I first met him. My life after that meeting has been very different from the first 30 years of my life. He came into my life that evening and in that one moment of meeting him, my whole life changed.

It happened like this. I had had an argument with my husband Nick, and in frustration I left my house and drove to one of the few places where I find peace, the Barnes & Noble Book Store on Kendall Drive. This was one of my favourite hangout places. This was where I felt comfortable; where I knew the people; this was where I would go every once in a while to seek peace amongst the many books, the many pages of knowledge and experiences of others.

I was at my favourite section—the self-help/inspirational section of books. I had pulled up a stool and was sitting down, thumbing through two or three books. I don't know whether he had been waiting there for me or had just walked in after me. But he came up behind me and said, "Hi."

I turned my head and looked back. There was a man about six feet tall, chunkily built, dressed in Levi's and a casual shirt, smiling down at me. He had very short hair which was slightly grey at the temples. He had large, broad shoulders, a large chest and I remember clearly that he was wearing boots.

He was smiling down at me, and in that smile there was some sort of a pull. I did not know him. I had never seen him before, but out of courtesy I replied back, "Hi."

"What are you looking for in these books?" he asked.

When I did not reply, he said, "All these books are useless for what you need—none of them is going to change your life for you. You are just wasting your time here."

To listen to all this from a stranger was not something I was accustomed to. Immediately, my defences were activated. I turned around and asked him, "So, are you trying to tell me that all these books here, in this particular section, which are supposed to change people's lives, are useless?"

He smiled again and replied, "That is exactly what I am telling you."

"How the hell do you know?" I asked.

"Oh! What language! See how easily you are angered. I am sure you have read a lot of such books before, haven't you?" he said. "So how come you don't have any better control over your anger than you did six months ago? These books are good no doubt. They are written by people who have had these experiences. It is their knowledge that you are reading about. But these books can help you only to the extent that they can make you aware of how other people changed. These are just descriptions of how those changes came about. Now they ask you to change in the same way. But the reality is that one cannot change like any other person on this earth. Each one of us is an individual different from the other, and the most these books can do is inspire you to *want* to change yourself. That is the sole end of these books. None of these books is going to change you without you changing yourself. All they can do is try to light a small spark of inspiration inside your heart which will then bring about a tremendous change, and let me tell you one more thing: the change will have to come when your heart also decides that you need to change, not only your mind."

"You seem to know a lot," I said. "And who are you that you have so much knowledge?"

"Who I am is not important," he replied. "What is important is who you are. Do you know who you are? Do you know what you are? Do you know why you are here today? And do you know why I am here today?"

"I don't really care," I answered.

"Do you care about your life?" he asked.

"Of course, I do."

"Well, then, I am here to make your life better."

"I don't need you to make my life better. My life is fine just the way it is."

He laughed loudly when I said this and said, "Then I guess I am wasting my time and I had better leave." He turned around to go and added, "If your life is fine just the way it is, and you are happy with it, then I guess you don't want any kind of improvement at all. Why did you call me here then? Why are you wasting my time?"

"Me, wasting your time? I didn't call you. I saw you here for the first time. You are the one who said 'Hi' and I just replied in politeness. That's all I did and now you are blaming me for you being here!"

"I am not blaming you for anything. In fact, according to me, you are not to be blamed at all for anything that is happening in your life because you are not aware of who you are. And of why the things that are happening to you are happening. You are as yet not aware of awareness. But that's okay, because this stage too is part of your growth and progress. Just look at your life as it is now. For a moment, stop to think about your life. You are so miserable with the way it is, you are so completely fed up. You often visit this section in this store to find peace and a way to change your life. And today the way is standing in front of you and because you are not ready to admit that your life has become so bad, you are trying to neglect this way. You are trying to ignore what you need. Your defences are saying that your life is as fine as it could possibly be. Even when help comes to you, your defences come up and stop the help from helping you. Can't you even see that? Come on, Cathy, come and have a cup of coffee with me," he implored.

I was not too sure I wanted to go with him for a cup of coffee. How did he know my name?

"Come on," he said. "There is a coffee shop right here in the store. Isn't it fantastic! A bookstore, with so many good books, such a fantastic place to be in, and then they go and open a coffee shop so that we can actually sit and enjoy a cup of coffee and read books at the same time. Come on, Cathy, take a risk once in a while."

Well, in any case, that was how our first meeting took place.

And you know what I did? I took the risk. I had a cup of coffee with him.

I don't know why I did it. Could be because I was angry at Nick, could be because I was frustrated and had left the house in that mood. And when he told me all that he did, I was tempted to find out more. Or it could be just because I knew we were in the store. We were not going anywhere where he could take advantage of me. I knew that I would be safe, no matter what, and I would have a choice of getting up and leaving. But whatever the reason, I remember that I said, 'Yes'.

He led me—or rather we walked together to the coffee shop—found a table and I sat down. He ordered an iced cappuccino for himself and asked what I would have. I said "The same," and waited while he brought the drinks to the table.

"I know you are still wondering as to who I am and what I am doing here. Let me tell you that right now before this relationship begins. Let me make that clear so that your mind is at ease. It is you who have brought me into your life. It is you who have called me here. I have been sent, yes, that's true—but it is you who have called me. For years and years, you have led a life which really was not the way you would have liked it to be. During these years, you have blamed yourself for your mistakes, you have blamed others for making you miserable. You have blamed circumstances for not allowing you to be happy. But try and remember, unconsciously or consciously, there has always been a call from your heart and your mind that you seek a better life and that you need help in creating it.

"Help me God, help me God! Do you remember that call over and over again? Do you remember your heart calling over and over again, when all the crying was taking place, when all the hurt and pain was taking place, do you remember your heart saying these words? These three words, Cathy, 'God help me' are as beautiful as 'I love you'. They are equally powerful and, believe me, they are from the same source. They are from the deepest, most sincere portion of your heart. When these words come up from their true source without any restrictions or blocks, there is nothing in this world or this universe which can limit their power."

I was not sure if I really wanted to agree with what he was saying. I did not remember my heart or my mind or anything of that sort calling out any words of any kind. But he was speaking with so much authority and totally believed in what he was saying that I just could not say no. But I didn't say yes either. I just kept quiet. I thought, let me wait and see where this conversation leads, let me see what he does next.

I noticed that he did not put any sugar in his coffee. He drank his iced cappuccino just the way it was, bitter, with no addition of anything else. He took a sip from his glass and said, "There comes a time in everyone's life when one needs a little help in overcoming certain obstacles which are inside us and which we ourselves can't see. For you, Cathy, this is one of those times and that's why I am here. If you want to change the rest of your life, if you want to become a happier person, if you want to be more content, to live life more fully than you are doing now, to have better relationships, if you want to love better, feel better and be better in everything that you do, say 'Yes' now. Say, 'Yes' to me, have faith in me and believe in what I am going to show you and tell you. All I ask for in return for changing your life is nine and a half weeks of your time; that's all I ask for. Give me nine and a half weeks of your time and I will change your life for you. In fact, for the first time in your life, I will give your life back to you. So, what do you say, Cathy, are you willing?"

So far, apart from my initial defensiveness and responses to him, I had been a listener. But now this was a question that I had to answer one way or another—yes or no. I had to because he had stopped talking. He was looking me straight in the eyes and waiting for my answer. And I didn't know what to do. His mention of nine and a half weeks brought to my mind a movie of the same title. This movie was about a relationship between a man and a woman who meet by chance, and nine and a half weeks are spent together in a very intense and explorative sexual relationship. After nine and a half weeks, separation takes place because both people start losing touch with reality and seem to be losing their balance.

"No, I don't mean nine and a half weeks like the movie, Cathy. There is going to be nothing sexual about this relationship. But yes, certain results will be the same as they were in the movie. You will begin to see reality in a completely different way. You may lose your balance for some time. Only if you lose your balance sometimes do you know where the real balance lies. The way you have been living your life so long, where is the balance? I promise you this though: it is going to be a completely safe and secure journey. There will be many changes, but they are necessary. The timing is crucial, so don't delay, don't delay change and don't delay your decision. Come on, yes or no, I want the answer right now."

I don't know why, but once again I said "Yes". I don't know what prompted me to make the decision. I found it particularly unnerving that he knew I was thinking about that movie at that time. Why was it that this strange man had met me in strange circumstances and was talking about strange things about which he should not even have known? I mean, what did he know about my life?

Or maybe it was because at that time I felt: 'Let me at least try it out. And if I don't like where it is going or what is happening in my life, I can just leave, I will just drop the whole thing and I'll leave. This is not a one-way street. I can get into it and get out of it any time. So, why not try it out? My life is bad enough as it is. Why not take a chance to try and make it better?' Maybe that was what made me say 'Yes'. Or maybe, it was just the faith and the belief that I could see in his eyes. When he was speaking to me he really seemed to believe what he was saying. Maybe that's why I said "Yes". But say "Yes" I did, and this is a story about what happened after that.

"So, what else do you know about me, apart from the fact that my name is Cathy and that I am not happy with my life, the way it is now? First, tell me how you know all these things," I asked him.

"I know all this because of the simple fact that I have been sent to you, Cathy. I follow higher orders and I have been ordered to come here in your life at this point of time and to show you just what life is. I know what you have been through, I know what you think, I know what you feel, and I know how you would like your life to be. I am here to show you the way, the way to be a better, happier and a more complete human being. I am going to show you what it means to be a woman? Now, isn't that paradoxical," he laughed, "a man showing you what it means to be a woman? But just have faith and I will."

"You claim to know so much about me, but I know nothing about you. What is your name, for instance? What do people call you?"

"The name that I have chosen to keep is Suraj."

"Suraj? That's a funny name. I have never heard it before. What does it mean? Where does it come from? And who gave you that name? Where are you from?"

"So many questions, Cathy! But I am happy to see that you are inquisitive. I believe you have a famous proverb in your language: Curiosity killed the cat. The proverb is true, you know, but very few people seem to understand its true meaning. Curiosity did indeed kill the cat, but it killed it in the sense that it could not continue to live its life any longer the way it used to. It was as if being curious had led the cat to knowledge, and that knowledge had killed the cat to the way it was before and given it birth again into a completely different world, into a completely different plane of existence. All of a sudden, because of this surge of knowledge, the cat's outlook, the cat's attitude, the cat's eyes, the cat's way of seeing things, of feeling things, everything was completely changed. So, the cat died and was literally born again into a completely new plane, in a different light and a completely new life. In any case, that is what the spiritual interpretation of the proverb 'Curiosity killed the cat' is.

"But let me not get carried away now, Cathy. Let me give you a few answers to your queries. I am called Suraj and that's the name I choose to keep. It has a meaning but I shall explain that to you later. Have patience. I am Indian by origin, meaning that I was born in this lifetime in India. But my true origin is the same as the true origin of each and every human and living being in this plane of existence. That is God. I have originated from God. But in this lifetime I have chosen to be an Indian.

"Where am I from? I don't know anymore because I travel all over the world and every place that I stop I feel is home to me. I identify with all kinds of people in the world, all different nationalities and races. I feel their pains and their happiness. I feel their sorrows and their pleasures. You could say that I come from this world."

"But do you have a family? Where are your parents? Where do you live?" I asked.

"Yes, I have a family; my family is humanity, each and every human being is part of my family, because we are all children of the same God, Cathy. Are we not? What makes you feel that you are any better than the other person? Look around you, look at all these people sitting around you. All these people reading books or standing or walking around you in this bookshop. Expand your consciousness, expand your vision for a moment. See the city of Miami, see the state of Florida, thousands and millions of people, see this entire country of the United States. Expand more. See this whole continent, see this whole world. How many millions and billions of people all around you. Different ages, different races, different nationalities, different beliefs, different faiths and still the deepest desires of all of them are the same, the deepest sorrows are the same, the deepest joys are the same. The deepest fears are the same too.

"So what makes you think that you are any better or any lesser than anyone of them? The truth is that we are all brothers and sisters and that the elder brother cannot be better or worse than the younger one. They are just at different levels of growth. Yes, I do have a family. My true family is all humanity. But once again in this lifetime I have chosen a wife and I have two children. My parents— they too are alive.

"Where do I live? Well, at present I am living in a motel room, but hopefully it is not going to be for a long period of time—and I pray that it will be only for nine and a half weeks, like I told you. Now, Cathy, enough about me. I think the hour is late now and you had better get back home to your husband. I am sure he will be eager to know

where you have been. He is waiting for you to
come back home safe and sound."

"You've got to be joking, Suraj. Just before
I came here, I had a fight with my husband.
That is one of the reasons why I came to the
store—I find peace and happiness here."

"Now wait a minute, Cathy. You can't find
peace and happiness here. You will find peace
and happiness only inside yourself. It is just
that when you are in this place, it is easier for
you to get in touch with yourself. It is easier
for you to go inside and find the happiness
and peace that you are looking for. This place
quietens you, this place calms you down.
This place is an inanimate location. How can
something inanimate give you peace and joy?
This place is not happy by itself. How can it
make you happy? Can somebody give to
someone what one doesn't have?"

"In any case what I was trying to tell you
was that I don't think my husband really
cares where I have been. I don't think he is
waiting for me to come back home," I said.

"Why don't you just go home now? And
please know for sure that your relationship
with your husband is something which we are
going to tackle in the coming nine and a half
weeks. So don't worry about what happens
today. When you go home, just accept
whatever happens. If he smiles, accept it and
if he argues with you, accept that too. Just
don't let it get inside you and disturb you.

Know that the future will be better. Have faith in that, have belief in that. So return home now, and I shall see you tomorrow. By the way, what about your job?"

"I am working with a clothing company."

"What I want you to do, Cathy, is to take leave for three months. Do you think you can do that?"

"No way, Suraj. I'll lose my job."

"Then lose it. What is more important to you? You want to change your life or you don't want to lose your job? What is priority number one? There are two things before you. Pick one. Every moment of your life is a choice, Cathy. Come on. Make a choice, make a decision. Decide what you want to do."

"Well, I can apply for leave, you know, but I don't think I will get it," I said.

"Why don't you just do what you can do? What you can't do is not up to you. So why worry about it? Why think about it? Just apply for the leave and let us see what happens. If you do get the leave, it is fine. We will have nine and a half weeks. If you don't get the leave, that's okay too. Maybe the time isn't right yet. But the only way we are going to find out is when you actually apply and see what the result is. Okay?"

"Okay, I think I can do that much. I think I have chosen to give my life a chance. I don't think my job is that important. I can always find another job, you know, if the need arises."

"I am glad for you, Cathy. I will see you tomorrow. How about breakfast at 9 o'clock?"

"9 o'clock? Isn't that late for breakfast?"

"We are also going to be changing timings in your life, just for your information. And, what better day to start than tomorrow? What time do you usually get up, Cathy?"

"About 6.30 or maybe 7 at the latest," I replied.

"Well, tomorrow morning when you get up, I want you to walk outside and turn your face towards the sun and speak out loud, 'Dear God, I am happy to be alive today. I seek energy from You and from the sun. And I seek Your guidance in turning that energy into positive results.' That's all I want you to do between 7 and 9. No coffee before 9. As much water as you want to drink but nothing else. Meet me at 9 for breakfast.

"Oh, and one more thing. When you return home tonight, I want you to return home with a smile. I know your husband is there. I know you said you had an argument just before you left. But now that you have started on this journey, this is one of the first steps you have to take. As I explained to you earlier, it doesn't matter and I don't care what he does: I want you to go back with a smile. That's all I ask. Just go home, open the door and when you see him, smile. That's all. And whatever he does, don't allow it to get inside you and affect you, one way or another, good or bad."

"Goodnight."

One can't change like any other person! One must find one's own way and pace!

2

THE KNOWLEDGE
STARTS TO FLOW

I have to admit that I was feeling very apprehensive on my way back home. I had met a strange man called Suraj, which I thought was a very funny name at that time. I had met him under strange circumstances. I· had agreed to things which I didn't know the depth of, and I was going back home with half a mind of trying to do what he was asking me to do.

Nick and I had been together ten years. We had known each other right through college, fallen in love, gone out, or rather courted, as people today are used to calling that period, for just three months and decided to get married. Now when I think back, I don't know why I agreed to marry him. It was very evident to me after two months of living with him that we were not meant for each other. But by then it was too late. The social agreement of marriage had been gotten into and it was much more difficult to get out of than get into it. From that time till today I had blamed myself for things going wrong. I had blamed circumstances for not giving us happiness. I had blamed my husband most of the time for not understanding what kind of a woman I was, what brought me happiness. I had tried my best to make him understand but to no evident result.

The period just before my meeting Suraj had been a most trying period for me. There had been fights and arguments every day. Every small thing I tried to do was misunderstood. Everything, I am sure, that he tried to do I didn't understand. There was no love left anymore in the relationship. It was as if we were living together because we had been married and that was all. There was no understanding, there was no touching of hearts at all. There was no touching of minds either. We were existing on two completely different levels of existence. There was no connection anymore. Coming home in the evening had become a misery rather than a pleasure that spending time with my husband should have been. I am sure it must have been the same for him. Spending time with each other was not something to look forward to anymore. But we still continued to live together. He led his own independent life and I tried to lead my own; at the same time we were trying to live with each other under the same roof.

I never understood how our relationship would work out in the long run. While in the relationship, all the negativity which surrounded me robbed me of my long-term vision, of the ability to see the way it might be in the future. We were not doing anything concrete to survive or to revive the marriage. We were not doing anything positive to make it work. I think all we both were living on was the hope that, one day, by some unknown force, by some unknown understanding which may come into one of us, things would change and life would turn out to be good and happy, nurturing and nourishing for both of us the way a marriage is supposed to be.

But having been through so much so recently, it was very difficult for me to go home with a smile.

As I reached home and pulled up into the drive to park my car, I wondered one last time if I could do it—if I was strong enough to go back into the house to see the man whom I had left only a couple of hours ago in a huff, to go back and see him with a smile on my face regardless of what he may feel, what he may say or what he may be thinking.

As I parked my car and walked into the house, I decided that I would give it a try. How much worse could things get between us than they were already? So I opened the door and walked in. There he was, sitting, watching television with a bottle of beer in his hands. And as he lifted his face to look up at me, I forced a smile on my face.

"What are you smiling about?" Nick asked.

"Nothing," I replied.

"We had a fight and you left with a frown. You have been out for some time now and you come back with a smile. What have you been up to?"

"Nothing," I replied. "I just went to the bookstore. I am smiling at you for no particular reason at all. Can't I even do that, Nick?"

"Okay, okay. Let's forget about it," he said and went back to watching television, which was okay by me. I needed time to myself to try and understand what had happened to me this evening.

Now that I thought back, while we were sitting there having coffee, I had not even noticed what was happening around me. I could not recall the people sitting around me, what anybody was saying or what the surroundings were. And I am usually a very self-conscious person. I always notice the things and people around me—what they are doing, what they are wearing, what they are saying, who is behaving in what manner, what kind of expressions people have on their faces. I notice people's body language. But of the time I spent with Suraj, all I could remember was him, what he said, how he looked, what he did, the smallest move of his hand was clear in my mind. The way his lips moved when he spoke, the things he spoke about. It was as if someone had chiselled it on my mind. I think it was his whole personality which just overpowered me at that time.

I spent some time recalling each and every moment of that evening, while Nick continued to sit in the dining room and watch television. After that I decided to turn in for the night. I walked out of the room and said, 'Goodnight' to Nick with a smile, came back and got into bed. About ten minutes later there was a knock at the door and Nick walked in.

"Are you asleep, Cathy?" he asked.

"No, not yet," I mumbled. "What is it?"

"O... ah...," he was having trouble saying what he wanted to say. "... I just thought... well, what I'm trying to say is that I'm sorry I snapped at you when you walked in. I felt that you would follow that smile with a sarcastic remark, and I let loose before you could. I am sorry, Cathy, I apologise."

I could not believe my ears. This was very unlike Nick. He was the one to carry a grudge for days and days. He was the one who could be off-mood over a small, simple thing for two, three days at a time, and here he was apologising to me! Frankly, I felt very nice listening to him say it. So I sat up, looked him straight in the eye, smiled once more and said, "Thankyou. I am glad you came in and said what you did. Believe me, I didn't have any sarcastic remarks to follow that smile. I just thought that you have been my husband for so many years and the least I can do, even when we have an argument, is to smile. That's all. There was just the smile, there was nothing else behind it."

"Well, thanks again, Goodnight," Nick said, and with that ended the first day of the rest of my life.

The next morning, as was my regular schedule, I got up, washed my face, brushed my teeth and went out to make myself a cup of coffee. But then I remembered what I had promised Suraj. No coffee, only water. I had a glass of water, opened the door and walked out on to the porch. The sun had come up probably half an hour ago. I looked at it and spoke the words Suraj had told me to. To tell you the truth, I felt very stupid when I was doing that. Can you imagine the scene? Early in the morning, a lady in her nightgown, out on the porch, looking up at the sun, raising her arms and speaking aloud to herself. Even if nobody could actually hear what I was saying, the scene itself must have looked extremely stupid. But I did it none the less, because I had given my word to Suraj that I would. I came back in, took a shower and got ready. Nick was ready too by that time and had a cup of coffee in his hand.

"What's your plan for the day, Cathy?" he asked.

"Oh, I don't know. I think I'm going to wait and see what comes up."

"Aren't you going to work?"

"I will probably go in a little bit late and, by the way, Nick, I have been thinking of taking some time off."

"Some time off, for what?" he asked.

"I just don't feel like working anymore, you know. I need a break. I think I need some time off to myself, to really get back in touch with my feelings. I have very little time to myself nowadays to really think and ponder over things. I don't think this is good for our marriage either. That's why I'll go a little bit later and apply for leave."

"Do you think you'll get the leave?" he asked.

"I don't know, but all I can do is apply for it, you know. Whether it is approved or not is not in my hands. So I am just going to do what is up to me."

"You are talking strangely today. This is not the Cathy I know," he said.

"You hardly know me, Nick," I smiled. "It has been ten years together. Don't you sometimes feel we hardly know each other, because if we did, we wouldn't cause each other so much pain and hurt."

"Yeah, I guess, you're right. I'm off," he said, putting his cup down and getting up to leave. He walked over and gave me a peck on my cheek. "See you later, take care."

"Bye," I said.

I waited till Nick left and then got ready to see Suraj. I picked up my handbag, made sure it had all the essentials that I might need during the day, took the keys of the car and drove out to the Dadeland Mall, where I was supposed to rendezvous with Suraj. I was wondering whether he would even be there. Somewhere at the back of my mind I had a feeling that he might not show up. Maybe it was just a trick or a practical joke someone was playing on me. Or maybe he was trying to pick me up using a strange and irregular technique. I have been told a few times that I am good looking in a very pure and clean way. God knows what men mean when they say that. But what I take it to mean is that there are some men out there in this world who still find me attractive. Maybe Suraj was one of them. But I need not have worried because as I pulled into the Mall, I saw him standing there waving to me. I pulled up next to him and rolled down my window.

"So... Morning, Cathy. How was your night?" he asked enthusiastically with a big smile on his face.

Once again his face caught my attention. It was more like a child's face than a man's. The enthusiasm, innocence and the feelings that it expressed reminded me more of a six-year-old child than a grown-up man. How old was he? I didn't even know. So instead of answering him, I asked him, "How old are you, Suraj?"

"What a strange question to ask me first thing in the morning," he said. "But I must give you an answer. I am twenty-nine years old."

"Twenty-nine? That's all!" I was amazed.

"Why, is being twenty-nine a crime?" he asked.

"Twenty-nine! I don't believe it. That means you are younger than me. God, what am I doing here? Believing that you are going to change my life for me? I am older than you, for God's sake, Suraj."

"Cool down, Cathy, cool down. Age has nothing to do with wisdom. I am going to show you how these two things are separate. Age is just an amount of time that you have lived in this life. That's all. You can't judge people by how old they are. Tell me something — are all twenty years old exactly the same in their level of thinking? Are all thirty years old the same in their level of thinking? Aren't there some brighter than the others? So, how can you judge? You are telling me that you are not going to believe what I say. You are not even going to give me a chance to try and make your life better just because of a small, simple fact that I am younger than you in age, that I am younger than you in this lifetime."

"It is hard for me to believe you are only twenty-nine, Suraj. The way you have been talking, you know, I would think you are around forty years old."

"Well, do I look forty to you, Cathy?" he asked innocently.

"No, you don't look forty, but you talk like a forty-year old man or maybe even older, maybe even forty-five."

"You haven't even asked me to get into the car. Can I do that before we carry on talking?"

"Oh, I am sorry. Come in. Where are we going now?"

"Just drive down and let's stop anywhere. We can have a cup of coffee. I think you need that now, don't you?"

"I didn't have it this morning, like you said, and I am used to having it every morning. So, yeah, I mean, let's go and pick it up. It will be good."

"Keep going straight. We will stop at the first fast food place that we see."

"Okay."

"Coming back to what we were talking about, Cathy, how much a person grows is not dependent only on the number of years they have lived. It is dependent on a number of other factors too. The main factor is what the person's motivations are. You see, all of us grow up wanting to know different things about this world. For example, we all want to learn how things function. When we were children, we wanted to learn how planes fly. All things that are operational in this world,

we want to know their how and why. That is
common to us all. But there are some inner
feelings, some inner desires to know certain
things which are different for every person.
Each one of us has different motivations and
that is what is important because what you
are motivated by, you will seek, and what you
seek, you will find, and what you find, you
will follow. I have always sought the truth in
my life. I was never happy with accepting
what people told me was the truth without
questions, without debate, without any logic,
just accepting what people told me to accept.
I was never satisfied with that. I always
sought the one truth, the real truth for
myself. That is what has always motivated
me. That is why some people today say I have
grown faster than my years. Isn't that what
you are saying too?"

"That's exactly what I am saying."

"Cathy, look at it in a different way. The
reason I am here with you today, trying to tell
you how to change your life is because I have
become what I am and that includes growing
up faster than my years."

"Boy, you sure know how to turn things
around, Suraj, let me tell you that," I said.

"Well, that's what our life is about, turning
things around, Cathy. Your life is not going to
change by itself. It is only what you make of
it. Once you change the way you think, once
you turn things around inside you,

everything around you, everything outside will turn around too. But that change has to be made inside you first. Don't expect things around you to get better if you yourself are not changing inside, if you yourself are not internally making it better. Believe this."

We kept on driving till we neared a McDonalds and he asked me to pull in. We walked in and he ordered French fries and coffee while I ordered a whole breakfast which obviously included my first coffee of the day too.

"Tell me something, Suraj. A guy like you who is talking such high things, do you think that eating something like French fries for breakfast is really healthy?"

"Ha! Ha! Ha!" he laughed. "I am happy to see that you are becoming more aware already. At least you are aware of what mistakes I am making. But what you need to do, Cathy, is to turn this around too. What you need to do is to first see what mistakes you are making. Now, for one minute, let's forget about my French fries. Can we do that, please, can you just take these French fries out of your mind?"

I gave him a strange look.

"No, I see that you can't. In any case, even if you can't take them out of your mind, at least put them aside for a minute and let us see what you are having for breakfast—a cup of coffee, some bread with an egg in the middle and a piece of meat."

I had ordered a Mcmuffin with egg, cheese and sausage. I was not sure if this described my breakfast correctly.

"No, no, no, that is really what it is. That is just what you are eating for breakfast. No more, no less. Let me tell you, Cathy, that out of all that you have in front of you, the only thing really worth eating for breakfast is the bread and nothing else."

"What do you mean? Thousands and millions of people, every day, every morning, eat this for breakfast in the United States and other parts of the world too and you are trying to tell me it is no good," I shot back.

"Cathy, it is not an unknown fact that people in general are not eating the correct kinds of food at the correct times. Your own dieticians and physicians have been telling you that and trying to change you for years. But what they don't understand is that they can't change you. What they need to actually do is to make you aware of what harm you are doing to your own body by eating these things. That will motivate you to change yourself. But we will go into that another time. Tell me, how was your night?"

"All I can say, Suraj, is that it was not as I expected it to be. I did go back with a smile even though it was very hard for me to do so."

"I am glad, I am glad," he said.

"I walked into the house and forced a smile. There was no feeling in it, but I did force a smile."

"Carry on. That's okay. That is not bad for a first step. What happened then?" he asked.

It seemed he wanted me to recall the whole scene frame by frame. He was always insistent on this. He wanted to know exactly how things had happened, the facial expressions, the movements of people. He wanted everything to be recollected and told to him. I described to him exactly how my night had been and when I finished, he told me, "So, aren't you happier now?"

"I am happier now, yes, but I know it won't last. Things between me and Nick have been going downhill for many, many years now. It is not so easy to become happier in my relationship just because he spoke a few nice words to me."

"Cathy, slow down, slow down. Why do you think so far ahead? All I am talking about is this moment. Are you happier now?"

"Yes, I am happier now, but I don't know if I will be happier after one hour."

"Don't think about one hour later. Can you please just tell me, are you happier now? Yes or no? That's a simple question. And it is multiple choice, yes or no. Pick an answer."

"Yes, I am happier now," I said rather loudly.

"Well then, it has been worth it. The smile that you forced on your face was worth it. See what even a faked, forced smile can do! Can you imagine that when you smile from your heart, when there is a direct connection between your heart and your face, just how powerful that smile would be? Just how much it could accomplish?"

We finished our breakfast and went to his motel room. I could see that he was travelling with very little on him. There was a small holdall kind of bag which I guess held whatever he needed for this particular trip. It was strange to be in his room because there was hardly anything which one could identify with him. All his belongings were in that small bag. It was hard for me to believe that a person could live out of a small bag for nine and a half weeks.

"Cathy, I am going to ask you a question now, and I want you to really think before you answer. Take your time, there is no hurry. This journey is going to be slow and steady, ever forward, ever growing. There is no shortage of time. But at the same time, time is at a premium because don't forget we all have a limited amount of time on this earth. I am going to ask you a question now which will probably be the most important question for you to ponder on. And I want you to take your time and give me an answer as truthfully as you can."

"Go ahead," I said.

"What's the purpose of your life here, on this earth, Cathy?" he asked.

"What do you mean by that? What is my purpose? What exactly are you trying to ask me?"

"I mean it exactly the way I said it. What's the purpose of your life? Why are you living, Cathy? For what are you living?"

"I am living, you know, because... well I am living because, I am alive, I am here. So I have to live. I don't have a choice, I guess. I have a family, I have to take care of them and ah... that's why I am here. I have a job to do and I may have kids later on. I have to bring them up and that's it."

"Don't hurry, take your time. Think about it and tell me the answer."

"No, I have already given you my answer, Suraj. There is no question of taking more time. I have a family, I have certain responsibilities, I have certain duties to perform and I have to fulfil those duties. That's why I am living. That's my answer and I am not going to change it."

"Okay, okay. So, as I understand, Cathy, you are trying to tell me, that you are living because you were born and you grew up as a child, when you obviously realise that you didn't have any responsibility, and now that you are grown up, you have to live as there is no other choice for you. Since you are an adult, you have responsibilities and you are going to fulfil those responsibilities and your so-called duties. Am I right?"

"Yeah, I guess that's about it!"

"Well, Cathy, consider for a moment that there are inanimate things in this world too, things which have no life. So, why were you given a life when the others didn't get it? Why did you not come into this universe as, say, a stone, or even if you were to be given life, why didn't you come as a lower form of life, like a tree or an animal? Why did you have to be born a human being? Was it only so that you could perform your duties till your life ends? Is that all life is meant for? Only to grow up, to perform your duties which again are not given to us by God but which we build up for ourselves, and to die? Is that the only purpose of life, to spend sixty or seventy years in growing up, fulfilling our duties, living up to our responsibilities and then dying? That's a long time to do so little, don't you think?"

"What are you trying to say? I don't understand you, Suraj. What more could there be to life? I mean, okay, people may want to visit places, people may want to see certain things before they die, people may have certain desires to fulfil such as making a certain amount of money or buying a certain car or achieving a certain level of affluence, they may want to have certain relationships, I don't know, but I think that's about it. What else can life offer?"

"Will you recap for me your life as it has been till today?"

So I told him about my life, about my childhood, about growing up with my parents and my brothers and sisters. I did not remember too much of my childhood, but I told him whatever I could remember. I told him about my years in school and my years in college, about my boyfriends and girlfriends. I told him about how my mind had changed from stage to stage, about the emotions and feelings I had felt with different people, about times that I had been happy, about times that I had felt sad because of certain happenings, about times when people had hurt me. I even told him about the times that I had hurt people, intentionally or unintentionally. I told him about how I had met Nick, how we had got married and the ten years which followed. I told him about my whole life.

"Cathy, the purpose of life is known only to a few of the millions and billions alive today. And to understand it, you must first believe that life is the greatest gift that God can give you."

"What is this God that you keep talking about, Suraj? Where is this God? You are talking about God again and again, but which God are you talking about?"

"Cathy, you have yourself mentioned God's name many times recently."

"Yes, but that's just a way of speaking, nothing more."

"Okay, forget about God for a minute, even though in reality we can never forget about Him. Let's call Him the Universe, let's call Him the Eternal Power, let's call Him the Universal Force, Energy, whatever you want. Even if you want to call Him Jesus Christ, that's fine with me. I love Jesus too because basically they are all one and the same."

"Right now, I am most comfortable with calling It the Universal Energy!"

"We will call It the Universal Energy then. Cathy, the greatest gift that this Universal Energy can give you is life. Believe this! Now let me tell you something else. There are thousands and millions of different entities and beings at different levels of growth in this universe. But there has to be something which is common in all of them, for them to exist in this envelope of time and space, all together. That common thread is the Universal Energy. It is there in each one of us, at different levels, in different measures. Some have it more than the others, but each one of us has it. Every living and non-living thing, everything that you see around you has this Energy. Some are aware of It, some are not. Some have more of It and some have less. But that is the common thread running through all of us and linking us back to our origin. Cathy, this life that you have been given is just another stage in your evolution. No, I am not talking about your evolution as a human body because actually you are not evolving as a human body. From the day you were born, you start to die. The day you come on this planet is the day of your birth, but every day after that you are coming one step closer to your death. You are not going one step away from it. Do you follow what I say?"

I had to admit that what he was saying was making sense. Once we are born, every day we come closer to our death, we don't go away from it, that much I could understand. I nodded and said "Yes."

"So, Cathy, actually our bodies do not evolve. This body has been given to you for a particular purpose, the purpose being to house your soul, to give it a means to experience, to feel, to touch, to give experience, a means to understand, to sense and to respond. And the body performs this duty in the most perfect manner. But the body has a lifespan. It performs its duty till its lifespan ends and then the body has to be dropped. But through the body, the soul is learning, the spirit is learning."

"But how can my body and my spirit be two different things?" I asked.

"See, that is the first mistake. You are already identifying yourself with your body.

You are not your body, Cathy. Your soul is you, your body isn't. Your soul is merely living in this body. You identify with your body because that's what you see, that's what others see, that's what they respond to. It is through that that you respond to the outside world. That's why you identify yourself with this body with which you sense and feel. It is through your body that you give your emotions, that you live your dreams, and learn and grow. That's why you say 'My body' or that 'I, the body, am Cathy,' whereas actually it is the soul which is Cathy and nothing else. There will come a day when you drop this body, but it is only the body which dies, you will not die. And you will be aware of this at the time of your death. You cannot be aware of it today, but you must still believe it to be true."

"Now, hold on for a minute. This is too much for me to accept. You are trying to tell me that I am really not my body at all."

"What I am trying to tell you is that this whole universe is a classroom for the growth of your soul. And for the soul to exist in this classroom and to learn through this life that you have been given, you need a body. That's why when two people in love express their physical love to each other, the human body is formed which is then occupied by a soul which deserves that body and has the right to live through it in this plane of existence. Now, once the soul has a physical body, the body grows and with that the feeling, the emotions and the mind which the body possesses change, and through these changes your soul grows.

"There is no doubt at all that each one of us is growing and we are all eventually headed in the same direction. There is only one certainty in this universe and that is that one day we are all going to be enlightened and become completely aware of who we are, what we are, where we come from and what we do. That's the only certainty that we have. But each one of us is travelling at a different speed.

"This life is like a journey. Tell me what you do, Cathy, when you get on a plane for a long trip. Let's say you are travelling to the USA from India, like I did. You will have to get on the flight and it would depend on your ticket whether you would be travelling economy class, business class or first class. To buy your ticket in any one of these classes of travel you would have to have a certain amount of money. So, if you have enough money with you, you could buy a first class ticket and travel more comfortably. Now, once you know that you are on the plane and cannot get off midway, it is up to you just how you spend the duration of the journey. Are you aware all the time that you have to arrive at your destination, that that is your final goal? Or do you get so lost in this journey itself that you forget completely about the destination? Do you spend your time on the flight being friendly to others or just keeping to yourself? Do you spend time helping others or just helping yourself? Do you spend your time on your journey cribbing and complaining about what you don't have, what you cannot get, or do you see what you have and what has been given to you and make the most of it? Life is just like a journey. We are only given a certain amount of time on this plane of existence and just how we spend this life is up to us. You have been dealt a hand of cards. Now you cannot change those cards. But what you do with those cards is up to you. Become aware of the fact of what life is, what its purpose is. Its purpose, Cathy, is evolution, a growth towards freedom, towards the fulfilment and realisation of your soul."

"By the way, Cathy, I forgot to ask you. Did you remember to greet God and the sun in the morning? Tell me the truth."

"Well, yes, I did."

"And, how did you feel?"

"To be frank with you, Suraj, I felt pretty stupid. Nothing happened! I just stood there and I did what you told me to. But nothing happened."

"Nothing was supposed to happen, Cathy. You see, you have not spoken to God and the sun for so long that they don't take you seriously now. It will take some time for you to get through to them. Ha! Ha! Ha! I am only joking," he laughed.

"What do we do now?"

"Beep. Awareness check, awareness check," he said, mimicking the beep of the "security alert" of an alarm. "Yeah, that is what it is, Cathy. What have you learnt today?"

"What?"

"What have you learnt today, Cathy?"

"Let me see. I think,...."

"No, don't think, don't think at all. Just feel and speak. Close your eyes for a minute. Go to your heart and feel from there and speak. What have you learnt today? Don't think. I don't want you to use your mind to tell me what I have taught you. Just feel, because I want it to come from your heart. So, come on. Awareness check. What have you learnt today?"

"You have told me the reason why we are alive, the purpose of life and that what we eat for breakfast is not too healthy."

Suraj laughed. "Don't take that so seriously. A lot of Americans — and the number is growing every day — are becoming very conscious of what they eat. They have realised that it is their bodies which are being harmed, and each day they are becoming wiser to their intake of food. And, don't forget one more thing you have learnt today, Cathy:

do not correlate wisdom with age. Children
who are so young have so much to teach us, if
only we listen to them, if only we look at what
they do, if only we see their behaviour and see
it with an attitude of learning from it.
Children are very wise in how they behave, in
how they express their emotions, in how they
let go of things. And they are so young. If we
would remain like children throughout our
lives, but still be able to grow and live in this
world peacefully and be able to handle the
responsibilities which come our way, we
would be very close to the universal energy all
the time," he said with a smirk. "Well, I think
that's enough for today. What do you say,
Cathy? Are you full with today's dose of
spirituality yet, or do you need some more?"

On my way back home, I had the distinct
feeling that Suraj was able to know what I
was thinking beforehand, because many a
time he had answered my questions without
my asking them. A thought would come into
my mind and before I could verbalise it, he
would answer it or clarify it. I decided to ask
him about this the next time we met.

> *The only certainty in this*
> *universe is that, one day,*
> *we are all going to*
> *be enlightened !*

3

HINTS FOR THE TRIP

The next day when I met Suraj he was his usual self, dressed in jeans, a casual shirt, a pair of boots and a smile on his round and childlike face. He seemed to have a particular affinity for wearing jeans and I filed this too at the back of my mind. I thought I must ask him about it.

"How did you sleep last night, Cathy?"

"Quite okay, I guess."

"What do you mean—you guess? How did you sleep? You have to know how you slept."

"I slept all right, Suraj, just like I usually sleep. You know, it was not anything good or bad. I just slept."

"Cathy, you must understand that the body is like a machine. This machine works on energy and each person carries this energy within him. And, occasionally, the body needs to be energised. It needs to go back to the source and receive energy. It is just as if you take a battery and charge it. And God has made it such that whenever the human body is stressed or feels tired, or expends a certain amount of energy it automatically reverts to its original source to receive more energy, and that is what we call sleep. Sleep is almost a form of meditation, except that sleep is involuntary and meditation is voluntary. Sleep depends upon a lot of external factors whereas meditation does not depend upon any external factor. And your sleep can be disturbed without your control but in meditation you can remove all disturbances if you have control.

"But, in its own little way, sleep is like a deep state of meditation where you go back to your source and draw energy from it, the difference being that in meditation you are aware that you are there, what you have to do. All these things come intuitively to you. And in the state of sleep you are completely unaware and you have no control over what is happening."

"Suraj, you seem to know a lot about all these different states and it makes me feel that you must have been through these yourself to speak with such authority on them. I want to know a little more about your life. Why don't you tell me more about yourself, Suraj?" I said.

"That is not important right now, Cathy. Maybe later."

"I have been meaning to ask you: I feel that somehow you seem to know whatever I am thinking. How do you do it?"

"It's like this, and listen to my words carefully. There is nothing new and there is nothing old in this universe. Everything just is. Nothing is created and nothing is destroyed in this universe. Everything just is. Everything just changes form. That is just about it. Things don't have to be this or that. They can just be. Can't they? Take yourself, for example. Why do you have to be a particular kind of a person? Why can't you just be? You change shapes and you change forms. When you are born, you are a daughter, and you are a child. You grow up, you become a teenager. You grow up some more, you get married, and you become a wife. You grow some more and you have children, and you become a mother. Then you may become a grandmother, and finally you die. But behind all this is the same soul which has existed, which is always going to exist and even when you leave this body, it is not dead.

"It is the same with knowledge. All knowledge has always been in this universe, including knowledge in terms of what people discover, what people invent, what people realise and what people solve.

"The universe functions on vibrations. Everything, as even the physicist will tell you, is vibrating at different frequencies. Take a cube of ice and leave it out in the open. After some time it becomes water. What has happened is that the energy which is in the cube of ice is now energy expressed in the form of water. The vibrations of the cube of ice have changed and become water because it has been influenced by external factors. The form changes but water remains the same. What it is made up of remains the same, remember this. Because of external influences the vibrations of this particular item have changed. The molecules have expanded and it has become water. Leave the water out for some time. Again because of external influences, the vibrations of this small quantity of water change. The molecules expand even more and the water becomes gas. But where does the gas go? The gas is still there as moisture. Where does the moisture go? It is still there in the air. Influence it more by external factors and it may come back again in the shape of ice. So you can see how forms change. It is all a change of vibration which changes your form.

"It is the same with knowledge. Like I told you, the physicist will also confirm the fact that everything is vibrating, including solids, liquids, gases and so too the human body. Our molecules are held together so closely that we are able to see each other. The atmosphere is vibrating too. It is just that the molecules are so far apart that we cannot see them. It looks like gas to us. We know it is gas, but we cannot see it.

"What happens is that when a person is born, he is born with a certain level of consciousness, a certain level of thinking and a certain vibration in his body. As the body houses the soul, the vibration of the body is in direct connection with the evolution of the person's soul or consciousness. As the person's consciousness evolves, so the body's vibrations change. As the body's vibrations change, or the range of vibrations grows, the human being becomes more perceptible to vibrations of other kinds already existent in this universe. If he is himself able to receive a larger range of vibrations, then he can obviously follow and understand anything in that larger range of vibrations present in this universe.

"You may have heard of people having miraculous powers as they become closer and closer to God. Actually, what is happening, Cathy, is that as their level of vibration is changing, their level of consciousness is rising and they are coming in touch with many different kinds of knowledge which comes to them intuitively. They just become receptive. They become like a radio which has a wide range of frequencies that it can pick up. And, once you become receptive, all this knowledge and different abilities come to you. So this is just one of the abilities that I have been fortunate enough to be blessed with," said Suraj.

"So you can read my mind?" I asked.

"Yes, at times I can read your thoughts and I know what you are thinking. But I don't do it all the time. It is not that sitting here I can figure out what millions of people in the world are thinking at the same time."

"Then how does it work?" I asked.

"You see, one of the important factors of life is focus. Nothing in life works without focus. It is just as in business. You may think, what does he know about business, when he is talking to me about matters of the spirit and the soul's evolution. But, believe me, I know more than you think I know. What happens in corporations? The key stress, the key factor, is focus: what the company focuses on—what kind of products it wants to make, what kind of market it wants to capture, what kind of quality it wants to put out. All these things are achieved only by focus. A General in the Army is able to defeat his opponent only when he is completely focused on his job.

"In the same way, in the spiritual field, in the spiritual life, in your inner life, focus is very, very important.

"I am able to use these abilities any time I want, but it is only what I focus on that these abilities are used on. I don't use them all the time, because I don't have the need to do so. The only permission I have been given is to use them when it is beneficial for bringing others closer to God. So I use it only during those times. But let's not go too deep into them just now. I will explain it to you later when it is appropriate," he said.

"But I want to know more about your life, Suraj. I think it will help me in my growth. Don't you think so?"

"There is a time for everything, Cathy, and when the time is right I am sure you will find out more about me. But right now, it is your life we are talking about. Now that you have started on the spiritual journey, this journey of your soul, of your inner being back towards its home, back towards its Father, back towards where it came from, one of the first things you must understand is that you are not allowed to carry any excess baggage on this trip.

"You know that when you travel international on any airline, you are only allowed to carry a certain amount of baggage. You are penalised for any extra weight over and above that allowance. The reason for this is that if you carry extra baggage, you make it more difficult for yourself to travel. You are not as free, and your baggage may hamper others on the way. As everybody has a certain allowance, your excess weight may actually cut down somebody else's allowance. So they charge you a penalty.

"Well, it is the same on this journey that you are on now. No excess baggage is allowed. The lighter you travel, the easier it will be for you. The lighter you travel, the less things you carry with yourself, the easier it is for you to move, to change and to grow. What I mean by excess baggage is that I don't want you to carry any grudges or any hatred in your heart. I don't want you to carry your troubles, or your bad feelings or judgements for others with you.

"Once again we come back to what I told you earlier: that is, that everything has energy. Even your thoughts have energy, even your words have energy, even feelings and emotions have energy. Just imagine how much energy of feelings patriots have inside them. Soldiers who feel patriotic towards their country are willing to give up their lives. The feeling which is created inside them is so full of energy that they are willing to give up their lives fighting for their country and for a cause they believe in.

"The feelings of love—when you feel love towards your children—imagine how much you can do for them. Where does that energy come from? A mother who sees her child being crushed under a car all of a sudden finds so much energy that she is able to lift the car and save her child. Later, she does not know where the energy came from and she is not able to repeat the feat. It happened instinctively, impulsively and the energy was provided by the feeling of love which came from the bottom of her heart. So, feelings and emotions have energy and the negative feelings of hatred, of pain, of grudges tha⁺ you carry with you, will have negative energy which will bring you down," Suraj explained.

"But you know it is very difficult to give up all these things just because you are telling me to do so. If I think back on my life, there are instances where I have been hurt, and there are people whom I blame for those instances. There are people who have hurt me and I still don't particularly like them. People have intentionally done wrong to me and I do hold some grudges against them. It is not so easy, Suraj, to give up all these things just because you are telling me to."

"Cathy, the first step will be if you are willing to give them up. I am not telling you to drop them right now. If you are willing to give them up, that is enough for now. But be willing, sincerely, because if you are willing sincerely, then everything around you will help you to give up these things. Everybody makes mistakes in life, okay. If somebody made a mistake or you made one and hurt somebody else, or even if things have happened in your life due to which you have given negative feelings about yourself to someone, or you carry negative feelings about someone else inside you, then stop for a minute. Go back and feel, go back and think what it was that created this. Learn from it. If you can solve it or improve it, find the way to do it, and, if not, then just let it go. Learn your lesson and let it go.

"These are two steps through which you must filter whatever happens in your life. First, don't keep thinking about them in your mind. What I told you was to think on them, think on these things, try to get your lesson out of them. Second, let it go after the lesson is learnt!

"Everything in this world that happens to us from the moment we are born till the day we die is meant for us to learn from; it is meant to teach us, to point us towards the reality of our own selves. This world is a big classroom, that is all it is. Every small thing is meant to teach us. When God gave us this body, this mind, this heart, the soul and the senses, when He gave us this whole human package, one of the greatest boons we were given along with it was the ability to take the smallest external input and to make it into the greatest internal growth possible.

"Cathy, only humans are capable of that. That is why, we are God's chosen ones. We are closest to Him. We are built in His own image. You have read the *Bible*. We are the children of God. We are all made in His own image. Jesus said, 'I am the son of God.' At that time, people did not believe him. But from what I have learnt and seen, we are all His children. And you shall see it too further along this path. We are all part of Him and we are all in His image. We are eventually going to merge back with Him, to realise ourselves.

"But remember these two principles: Whatever happens in your life is meant to teach you, to point you towards God. It is meant to make you grow. You are supposed to learn something from it and then to let it go."

One of the greatest gifts we have is the ability to take the smallest external input and to turn it into the greatest internal growth possible!

4

WHY GET STUCK?

"Whether good things or bad things happen to you, don't get carried away. When things are good, don't feel too elated because you know that a day will come when you will feel sad, and when things are bad, you have to learn from those too. Just don't get into the trap of thinking: why are these bad things happening to me? What have I done wrong? Why are people doing this to me?

"These are all negative thoughts that your mind will get trapped in. Instead, you have to think 'This thing has happened to me. I feel pain, hurt, dejected, I feel let down but something is there that I am supposed to learn from this.'

"Once you identify that, learn that lesson and then let it go. Drop the thing. Don't get stuck in it. Life has progressed already. Whatever has happened to you is in the past, it is not present anymore. Every moment going by is in the past. So you've got to carry on and go beyond it. Don't get stuck in the past. Don't keep thinking about the future either. Be in the present. And, remember: when you are facing a good thing, be happy, but know at the back of your mind that tomorrow you may be sad. When you are feeling sad, know that tomorrow you will be happy. Everything shall pass. And it is now time for me to tell you a small story. Would you like to hear it?" Suraj asked.

"Sure," I replied.

"One day, a long, long time ago, there was a rich king who ruled over a rich land. He had great armies, a wonderful family and a large kingdom. And this king was motivated by the growth of his soul as much as by the growth of his kingdom.

"All was well in his kingdom, so he decided to appoint a Committee of Wise Men. He called the ten wisest men in his kingdom to come and form this committee and guide him on spiritual matters. This spiritual committee would read daily to the king, explain spiritual lessons to him or interpret the scriptures for him. They would tell him how to get closer to God, what paths to follow, what meditation techniques to use and even what saint was visiting the kingdom so that the king could meet and learn from him. All this carried on for years and years."

"He gained a lot of knowledge, I guess," I said.

"You know, Cathy, there is no dearth of spiritual literature or spiritual books in this world. In any case, after years of listening to his wise men daily for hours, one day the king got frustrated and called an urgent unscheduled meeting of his committee. He sent out his soldiers to their houses to inform them that the king was summoning them for an urgent meeting. That they must drop everything and come straight away.

"When each of these wise men got the message, he started wondering what it was that was disturbing the king so much. 'It must be a big spiritual dilemma the king must have got into that he needs us so suddenly,' each one thought.

"So, they rushed eagerly to meet the king. He told them that he had been listening to them for years and years every day for hours on end. 'You have read to me from every religion in this world,' he said. 'You have taught me the teachings of the wise men and you have interpreted the scriptures for me. You have told me the different paths to follow which lead to the same goal. But too much knowledge has made me confused. Too many ways have made me uncertain. One thing I am sure of though, and that is, a man when he is truly wise does not feel low, dejected, and sad when bad things happen, and does not feel elevated, elated and high when good things happen to him. I know that a wise man is always in a state of equanimity. He is in the same state whether good or bad things happen because he knows that God is in control of everything, good and bad, and they are just meant to teach us.

" 'Now, when I am going out to fight a battle, when there is death all around me and my mind is working only on how to survive, when I have a sword in one hand and a shield in the other and am fighting to save my life, do you think that I can remember or recall all these big scriptures that you have read out to me. No! So, what I want you to do,' he said to the Committee of Wise Men, 'is to give me a small one-sentence formula that I can remember always and which will keep me in a state of equanimity. When good things happen to me, I should not get carried away and when bad things happen to me I should not feel depressed. Give me one formula and that formula should contain the condensed wisdom of all the scriptures. Be sure you make it such that it keeps me always in a state of equanimity.'

"This was his command to his committee. And, before they left, he added, 'If at the end of seven days you do not have such a formula for me, then I shall accept the fact that you are not wise men and I shall chop off your heads for having tried to fool the king.' With that he ended the meeting."

"What happened then?" I asked.

"That was the day the real worries started for the group. They held meetings after meetings, and talks after talks, and they condensed their collective wisdom down to ten chapters. Each one of them contributed one chapter. When they talked to the king, he said it was too long. 'I don't want ten chapters, I want one line,' he said.

"So they made the ten chapters into one chapter and he still refused it. They made the one chapter into one paragraph and he still refused it. By now six days had gone by. In desperation, the group of wise men went to the forest where a seer meditated and lived occasionally. They were lucky enough to find him. They told him of their predicament. Without hesitation the seer took a piece of tree bark, wrote down one sentence and gave it back to the wise men who then took it to the king and told him they had the answer."

"So what was the answer?"

"The king was very happy that finally they had been able to condense all their wisdom into one sentence. He asked them to tell him the sentence which would always keep him in a state of equanimity.

"And, you know what the sentence was, Cathy? Four words only, but if you follow these four words sincerely, nothing in life will truly disturb you. These four words were: THIS TOO SHALL PASS!

"This too shall pass! That was the sentence which contained the wisdom of thousands and thousands of years, and of all the scriptures of different religions.

"The teachings, the ways and methods which we use to actually calm, quieten and stabilise our mind are given in this sentence of four words: THIS TOO SHALL PASS."

"If everything passes, Suraj, then what is really important?"

"The nature of everything in this world is transitory. That is important to remember, Cathy. Everything passes. The sun comes up in the morning, goes away at night. The moon comes up in the night, goes away in the morning. A child is born, sure enough one day he is going to die, just as surely as he is born. Something is dying, sure enough there is going to be regeneration and a new birth. A volcano bursts and wherever the lava falls everything dies. But, do you know what the scientists have discovered? Beneath that lava life is growing, and one day it sprouts out through that lava.

"Everything moves in a circle, and whatever comes must go, what goes must come. It is a circle, round and round, round and round. Everything in life is transitory. Good times happen to you, very good, enjoy them. But do not get stuck in them. They will pass. Bad things happen in your life, they will pass too. Just learn the lesson they offer.

"Just as water from the mountains flows to the ocean, we also flow towards our higher self. Everything in this life keeps changing. Everything passes. Constant change is the nature of this world and everything in it. All waters pour into the ocean and yet the ocean is itself always in a state of change through creation, preservation and destruction.

"And remember also that this Law of Transitoriness, of everything being transitory, also applies to your emotions and feelings. If one day you feel angry with your husband, don't get too caught up in that anger because you know that soon it will pass and tomorrow you shall not feel so angry with him. Even your emotions and feelings are subject to this law. So don't get caught in the feelings of anger, of hate, in carrying grudges against people or of getting even with people. Getting even, as you will realise later, does not balance things out. It throws everything out of balance because you have tried to disrupt something which had actually become in its normal balanced state. For now, remember this law of everything being transitory and the law that everything moves in a circle. Do you follow what I am saying, Cathy?"

"Suraj, you are saying so much, you know, that it is very difficult to just believe and accept everything as the truth."

"The truth is only one, Cathy, and that truth can only be known by experiencing it yourself. All I am doing is giving your a glimpse of it with words, but you shall know the truth only when you experience it. If I spend years talking to you about truth, it is not going to get through to you, but the day you have the experience of even a moment of truth, you will come to believe all that I am saying. So, I am only preparing the way for you to do the experiencing."

"How will the experiencing come to me, Suraj?"

"The experiencing comes from two things: one, self-effort in trying to make yourself ready, and second, the grace of God. When He is happy with your self-effort in trying to make yourself ready, He shall give you what you ask for.

"Okay. Beep. Awareness Check. Which two laws have I told you operate in the universe? Come on, quickly."

"The law of everything being in a circle, everything coming and going, everything without a beginning, without an end and the next law you told me, Suraj, was that everything is transitory," I answered.

"That's good. That's really good. Now what I want today, Cathy, is to expand on the law that everything moves in a circle. And, do you know where we are going? We are going back to the *Bible*.

"Do you remember what Jesus said? 'As you sow, so shall you reap.' I am going to explain to you later how that itself is a circle, and how every religion believes in it."

Things at home with my husband Nick were not really improving. We still had our differences, we still lacked understanding, and a touching of each other's hearts, emotions and feelings. Basically we were spending time together, but we were really not together. And I guess at that time neither of us was willing to take the first step and put out a compromising hand.

As a result, we carried on as we had for the last many months. We spent the evenings sitting on the sofa watching television. Nick would be in his own world, a bottle of beer in his hands. I would flip through a magazine, but my thoughts would be on what had happened to me during the day when I spent time with Suraj. All his talk and the logic that he was sharing with me was finally getting through to me. So far, anything he would say would come up against my outer defences and not get inside me. But now I detected a subtle change. I felt that whatever he was saying was slowly seeping into me. It was finding the empty spaces, the cracks and gaps within my outer defences and seeping in through them to the inner core of my being.

When I was with Suraj, I felt at peace, I felt protected, I felt that I was at the right place, completely comfortable and free—free to be myself, free to ask what I wanted, free to do what I wanted, free to express myself—all the things which I never felt with Nick. I knew what I was feeling for Suraj, the direction in which my feelings were going, was wrong. I should have been feeling these for my husband.

But the irony was that as soon as I came home in the evening, all feelings of peace, harmony, and being comfortable and open vanished. It was almost as if as soon as I was in the presence of my husband, our energies were completely conflicting and disturbing to each other. Thus, even though my life was changing when I was spending time with Suraj, everything returned to "normal" when I came back home.

With Suraj I felt that I was growing and opening up, that what he was saying was beginning to find a place inside me. It was beginning to touch my inner being, my heart and not only my mind.

'This too shall pass!'

(Remember that this also applies to your feelings and emotions.)

5

CIRCLES OF LIFE,
LIFE IN BALANCE

I don't know how the days passed by,
spending time with Suraj. When I was with
him, time seemed to fly.

He had rented a car and would take me for
long drives. We would drive for hours on end
while he explained different mystical and
spiritual concepts to me. He made me realise
the deep meaning in the most simple events
of life. He taught me to see the underlying
beauty in the most mundane of things, in the
most ordinary and normal things of life. He
taught me to recognise the hand of God
behind everything. I am not uncomfortable in
writing about God here because that is
something I came to accept after only a few
days of spending time with Suraj.

He told me that there was a time and
purpose to everything under the Heavens and
also pointed out that though this was written
in the *Bible* it was a universal principle,

which applied whether you believed in it or not.

"There is a time and purpose to everything under the Heavens," he said, repeating the words of Jesus Christ. "Not a single leaf falls if its time is not apt, not a single stone is upturned if it is not with God's will and God's desire." Going further on the same theme, he told me that there was also a time and purpose to our meeting each other, at this moment, in my life.

He made me aware of how my soul had been crying out for change, for improvement in my way of life, for harmony and peace. My spirit had realised that I had come to a stage where I was stuck and all my cries, conscious and unconscious, had built up a sort of critical mass. This mass then led to many changes and a chain reaction, which eventually resulted in Suraj coming into my life.

He told me again and again that the only reason why he had come into my life was to change the way I was looking at it, the way I was handling it, and the way I was giving in to it. He told me that he had come to give me new eyes, and to put me back in touch with my heart.

The time that I was spending with him was becoming more and more special. I wanted to spend less time alone by myself, with my husband, or with my friends. Ever since

meeting Suraj, my social life had almost come
to a standstill. My friends would call and I
would ignore their invitations. They wanted
to know the reason for this sudden change,
but I didn't feel like sharing it with them.

I was also becoming more and more
distant from Nick, and he could sense the
change. I told him about Suraj. I told him how
I had met this strange man on one of my
visits to the bookstore, of how we had got
around to talking and having a cup of coffee
while sharing thoughts on life and one's
spiritual growth in this lifetime. I told Nick
how much I was learning from Suraj and how
he was changing my views. I think all this
talk about Suraj made Nick a bit jealous. He
told me repeatedly not to get carried away by
strangers. He told me again and again that it
was a difficult time in our lives, each one of
us was having problems with the other, and
this was just the time when it was very easy
for someone from the outside to step in and
take advantage.

There was no way I could not accept the
fact that Suraj was trying to take advantage
of me. There was nothing he had asked of or
from me. In fact, ever since I had met him he
had been giving to me. He had given his views
on life, on God, on the universe, on a person's
duty in life, on a person's purpose of living
sixty to seventy years in this plane of
existence. All he had asked me for was a very

short period of time in my life. He had never asked for money or made any kind of material demands from me. The demands that he made were on my time, my emotions and my awareness, only so that he could use them to make me a better person. In any case, let me rewind a bit here and tell you more about the law that everything moves in a circle and how it evolves into the law of action and reaction.

Suraj had last left me saying that he would tell me more about Jesus's words, "As you sow, so shall you reap", the next time we met.

He started off by saying, "Cathy, I told you that everything moves in a circle. Scientists have now discovered that there are cycles to everything. In the ocean, there is a high tide and a low tide. Every time the low tide occurs, be sure that the high tide will occur after that, and every time a high tide occurs, be sure that the low tide will occur after that. Things go up and they come down and again they go up and they come down.

"Economists have now discovered that all the markets in this world move in cycles. There is a period when share prices and stock values go up, which then carries on for some time before the curve starts falling and it hits rock bottom. Then it moves up again. Things always move in a circle. This also holds true for what we do in life, and what we get back. In simple English, in the modern world, we say, 'You scratch my back and I'll scratch yours.' Jesus said it in a different way. 'As you sow, so shall you reap.' The Hindus call it the law of Karma: what you do comes back to you. Do good and good will come back to you. Do bad and bad will come back to you. It is that simple.

"All your actions or reactions to other people's action have a certain energy in them. Now, if you are putting your energy in good action, eventually the same energy will turn around and come back to you. If on the way that energy had helped anybody, then it becomes more potent and expands numerically before it returns to you. It is the same way with negative energy. We do something bad to somebody, it becomes more potent, and the stronger energy comes back to you.

"The only critical point here is that it may not happen instantaneously. There may be a lapse of time before it comes back to you. And that is why people have difficulty in understanding or believing in this law on a day-to-day basis. You may see a person robbing a bank, and nothing goes wrong till the end. He is successful, he makes his getaway with the loot and is never caught. You might think that he got away with it. But believe me nobody gets away with anything in this world.

"God is always watching, the Universal Force always keeps in balance what is good and bad about everybody; what is positive and negative. Who has done what, who has taken away whose rights, who has taken away whose ideas. Is one person taking advantage of another? All of these things are fixed in terms that if you do something, you know what is going to happen in return. Here is the circle again. You do something, it turns around and comes back to you. As it comes back to you, you do something again as a reaction to that, it goes out again and comes back to you.

"Now, how do you break through this circle? Because you are always under the control of cause and effect. Say, you do something. That is a cause and there is an effect to it. If you do an action, there is bound to be a reaction to that from somebody else, or something else. That reaction coming to you becomes an action and you again react to that action which is again a reaction. So the circle carries on endlessly, continuously."

"Isn't there any way to break this circle?" I asked.

"The only way to break this circle and to get away from this law of cause and effect, Cathy, is to have control over your actions and reactions, over what you do or do not do. Let us take a very simple example. Tomorrow, suppose someone close to you does something really bad to you which hurts you. At that time, reflexively you want to hurt the other person back. Because, over so many years, you have learned that if somebody hurts you, you should hurt them back. Doing so gives you momentary satisfaction. You feel, 'I taught them a lesson.'

"But if you stop for a minute and try and understand, try to be aware, it may be that what is coming back to you now is a result of something bad that you had done earlier on. And once you have that awareness, you have a choice. Do you want to do something bad in return, in which case the circle will go on forever? Or do you want to accept the bad that has come to you in the understanding that it is a paying back of the bad that you had done earlier? And thus, by accepting, without a reaction on your part, you break the circle. Do not take any action. Do not react to what has happened to you. Right then and there, the circle breaks. The accounts have been settled, you did something negative, the negative came back to you, that's it. Don't do any more negative.

"Now, once you are on the spiritual path, and as you become stronger, what you are supposed to do is that for every negative that comes to you, you have to give out a positive. Remember Jesus when he was crucified. Lord Jesus Christ was the son of God, just as we all are. He was fully aware, he was completely merged with his Father, but he knew he had a role to perform in this world. That was his only purpose of coming here. Even then the people around him betrayed him. They did not understand his value, they did not understand his message and they crucified him. We all know the pains and miseries that Lord Jesus Christ was subjected to. Even then, when he was being crucified, I am sure you know what he said, 'Lord, forgive them for they know not what they do.'

"Jesus Christ, who was obviously a very, very aware person, who was fully realised, was so strong that even when the worst of negatives were being thrown his way, he was doing something positive in return.

"No, I am not saying that we all start from that level. But yes, that is the stage we all reach eventually before we go back home, before we merge with God, before we find ourselves.

"Lord Buddha, who started the religion of Buddhism as we know it today, said that one must have complete control over one's actions and reactions because that is the only way to break the circle of Karma. Karma is a Hindu word, and, loosely translated, it means cause and effect.

"So, only if you stop your reactions to somebody's actions to you or you have control over your actions, i.e., anything that goes out of you, that is the only way to break the circle of cause and effect. Cathy, always remember this."

"But what about evening things out?" I asked.

"You are aware that in the material and mundane world that we live in, we are taught that 'An eye for an eye' is fair. This is true no matter what culture you are growing up in. Society generally teaches us to believe that when you get even with somebody, when you hurt them because they hurt you, when you do something bad to them because they did something bad to you, things are actually put back into balance. You have settled accounts. They did something bad to you, so you must reciprocate by doing something bad to them. And it is only after that that the score is settled and things are back in balance.

"Actually, Cathy, the cosmic law says that getting even puts everything out of balance. Now this is something which you should remember. This is something which you should use in your life. When things are going wrong in your life or things turn out in a way you didn't expect them to, always remember that getting even puts things out of balance from the cosmic point of view. You have to consider that what happened to you was necessary to put things back in balance, it was due to something you had done and that it was also happening for a reason.

"As I told you earlier, one of the laws was that everything has a reason and a purpose and a time. So the purpose for which this thing is happening to you is what you should concentrate on instead of why it is happening to you.

"Instead of trying to put things back in balance, which would actually be putting them out of balance, try and find the purpose, the benefit, the lesson that you can learn from this thing, this incident which has happened in your life. Take that lesson and pass on. Take that lesson and let go. Remember the lesson, don't remember what has happened to you. That is the way to fly through life.

"Everything in this world that happens to us, every small thing in our life is made to teach us and to help us grow and to become better, more loving, more giving and more harmonious individuals. However, in daily life, it is very difficult to keep this understanding in front of us all the time. To see every incident of our life through the filter of this understanding is extremely difficult. But the effort must be made by the aspirant. If you aspire to become a better person, this is the way to do it."

> *Just as on a trip, travel light and you travel fast, so too, on the spirit's journey any excess baggage will slow you down!*

6

HERE AND NOW!

"Well, Cathy, one more thing to go before we finish this day. Remember, earlier I was talking about Lord Buddha, the founder of Buddhism. He also gave us one more very important lesson."

"And what was that? Tell me," I said.

"Lord Buddha had realised for himself that in life, to be really alive, a man has to live in the present. He told us that life is not available to us in the past or the future. It is only available to us in the present moment. On a regular day, we have billions of people waking up in this world, and thinking that they are alive, feeling that they are alive, that they are truly living. According to Lord Buddha, none of them are living. They think they are living, but they do not know, what it truly means to be alive.

"Lord Buddha, through his own experience, understood the fact that all of us most of the time are either thinking of the future or pondering over the past. We are either ahead of ourselves in the future, or behind ourselves in the past. We are worried about things which have happened to us, what we have been through, what people have done to us, the circumstances that we have passed through. All of these things are in the past. Or we are worried about what is going to happen tomorrow. What will so and so say? What will she do? What will be my state after one year?

"Lord Buddha said that we spend our lives either in the future or in the past. We are not actually alive because we are not here right now. We are not present in this moment, which is the only time we actually have. Now if your mind is occupied all the time between the future and the past, what is left for you to be here with? Are you conscious of yourself right now? That you are here standing on your own two feet, living on this earth, conscious in the present moment? All of us have a habit, a tendency, to think either forward or backwards and not to be in the present moment.

"Lord Buddha clearly told us that life is available to us only in the present moment. All he wanted from us to become fully awake was to be completely here right now at every given moment of our lives. He said that if you are a hundred per cent present, in the present moment, every moment of your life, then where will you have the time to worry about the future or to fret about the past? Where will you have the time to worry about what is going to happen to you the day after tomorrow? He said, 'Be here fully right now in the present moment and everything else will take care of itself.' "

"Sounds pretty simple."

"In fact, this is an extremely difficult thing to do. To be completely here right now, to forget about everything else and to become fully conscious. Right now, right here, at this moment. To completely gather your consciousness from all the different directions that it is running away in, to focus it and to bring it down to the present moment. That is all that enlightenment means, Cathy. If you are able to do this, you become fully awake, you become fully alive, you become fully aware and fully conscious of everything there is in the universe."

"This is a very simple but a very powerful formula. You think it is easy. The fact is, it is not so easy to follow. But if you can do it, the results that will follow will be tremendous."

"Tell me more about Lord Buddha's life."

"Lord Buddha was born a prince. He had a very rich father, a whole kingdom at his disposal. When he was born, all the court astrologers told the father that the boy was destined to become great. But they added that either he would be great as a great king, who would conquer lands and expand his kingdom, or he would become a great saint, a very holy and realised person, who would teach people to become like him. He would give freedom to others in the world, they said.

"Lord Buddha's father named him Siddhartha, and decided to do his best to make sure that nothing in his son's life should lead or point him in the direction of a saintly life. He did not want any of his son's desires to remain unfulfilled. He wanted him to have the best of everything.

"The best that the father's resources could provide was given to Siddhartha. He had three palaces all to himself, each with more than a hundred rooms. He had a very beautiful, completely faithful and loyal wife. More than that, he was surrounded by all kinds of beauty ever since he was a young child. He had total freedom. He got whatever he desired. His father was also very careful that his son should not see any kind of disease, old age or misery prevalent in the world. So he always kept him inside these strictly controlled palaces.

"However, one day Siddhartha went out of his palace and was exposed to all these things. That was the day he decided that he had been wasting his life. He asked himself, 'What is the use of my living this life and trying to enjoy so much now, if one day my body is going to grow old and die? I cannot escape that. That is my inevitable end. Am I doing anything now to help me face that better?'

"And that question changed the direction of his thought and life. All his attachments to his senses broke down on that day. And Siddhartha went on to become a fully realised individual. He followed a lot of different practices, he tried a lot of different ways. After some very severe practices and penances he eventually found his own balanced, middle way.

"One day, when he was meditating, a rich merchant passed by. When he saw Lord Buddha meditating under a tree, he immediately recognised him to be a realised saint. So he waited till Lord Buddha opened his eyes, and then went up to him and asked, 'I know who you are. I have heard so much about you. People say that you are God, people say that you are a celestial being, people say that you are one of the angels who have come down to Earth, that you are the king of the whole universe. Tell me who you really are.'

"And do you know, what Lord Buddha replied to him? He said, 'I am awake!' That's all!

"Buddha means one who is awake, one who is completely awake. In saying this, Lord Buddha was implying that with all the knowledge and all material pleasures, with all the fulfilment of our desires that we run after in this lifetime, we are not truly awake. We are actually in a state of sleep, in a state of slumber. With our eyes closed, we run after the gratification of our desires, all momentary pleasures, without really realising the purpose of this life, without becoming conscious and aware of our own true selves. Our purpose in this life is the growth of our soul.

"That day, Lord Buddha, who had achieved the state of complete and full consciousness, at all given moments, of Universal God presence, in reply to the merchant's question, describing himself, said, 'I am awake.' That is all!"

"So a person who has realised is awake and we are not?" I asked.

"The difference between us and a realised person is that he is completely awake. He is completely aware."

"Awake to what? Aware of what?" I asked.

"He is completely conscious at all given moments of his life of his own divinity, and the divinity of others.

"He is aware of the purpose of this life, the purpose of every incident which takes place in life, the purpose of the senses that we have been given, the purpose of the mind, the heart, the soul, and the purpose of our relationships.

"He is completely aware of all these in his Universal Consciousness. Therefore, he is

completely awake. Not for one moment does
he fall out of this consciousness. Not for one
moment does he become not awake.

"Do you know that in India people
traditionally greet each other using a word,
'Namaste'? I did not know the meaning of this
word till it was explained to me by one of my
teachers. He told me that this word had
actually evolved from an ancient Sanskrit
phrase and meant 'The divinity in me greets
the divinity in you.' When two people on the
street meet each other, fold their hands in
front of their heart, and say 'Namaste' to each
other: 'The divinity in me greets the divinity
in you.' These two persons may be from
completely different levels of society, one may
be rich, one may be poor, one may be old, one
may be young. There may be a lot of
superficial differences between them, they
may not even know each other, but they do
know that divinity exists in both of them.
Divinity is the same in both of them.

"What a beautiful way of greeting each
other! Compare this with 'Hi!' 'How are you?'
'Hello?' 'How are you doing?' and see which
touches your heart most. The sad part,
Cathy, is that in India today, people use it all
the time without really understanding its
meaning, without becoming aware of what it
means. But, none the less, the original
thought, the original idea behind this

greeting was very pure. That we must not forget."

> *Trying to become happy*
> *from outside in is futile.*
> *Trying to become happy from*
> *inside out is fertile!*

7

CARDS AND ATTRACTION

I spent a few days digesting what Suraj had said before I met him again. I don't know what he did for those few days. I didn't ask and he didn't tell me.

"So what now, Suraj?" I asked.

"Whatever I've already told you is enough to change your life, Cathy," he replied.

"I know," I answered, "but you can't stop now and I still have some time left out of our initial agreement."

"What more do you want to know?" he asked smilingly.

"Tell me why some people seem to have good lives and why some of us only seem to have problems?"

"We all are responsible for our lives, for the way they are, whether we see it or not," he said.

"Yes, but how?"

"Cathy, in life there are certain things which are given. They cannot be changed. There are certain things which we come with, which we do not have a choice to discard or to give up and change for a better package. For example, you came through your parents. You have a certain body, a certain character and a certain upbringing. The way your parents brought you up is also very important because what the parents have become is what they pass on to the child when the child is growing up.

"There is a saying, 'The education of a child begins twenty years before it is born.' My master taught me that. What it means is that actually when the future mother is being educated, you are imparting education that the child will get, when it is born years later. Therefore, before the child is born, what the mother has learnt is as important as what the child will learn after it is born. But that is a lesson for another day. Let us get back on track now."

"That seems to be pretty important for women, don't you think?" I asked.

"It is. Remember it, but let's go back to where we left our talk," he replied. "I was telling you earlier that life is like a hand of cards dealt to you. Let us say, five people are sitting at a table. You have been dealt a hand of cards. Now, once you have the cards in your hand and take a look at them, you do not have a choice of changing them. However, you do have a choice of how you play the hand. Knowing what cards you have, just how

well you choose to use the capability of
bluffing, the capability of judging others, of
coming across to others, of showing your
confidence, or of making a wise decision that
this may not be a hand of cards that you want
to bet on. All these things are up to you. The
choice is yours.

"Many times in life it so happens that in
certain instances it is better to sit back and
let the other person have his way. That is also
a result of good judgement. It is poor
judgement to go on and on when you know for
sure that there will not be a positive outcome.

"What you come with is fixed. But after
you are here and you accept what you have,
there is such a wide choice open to you for
improvement, for making yourself better, for
learning more, for coming in contact with
people who are spiritually or mentally higher
than you and can help you to improve and
grow.

"In life everybody goes through both good
and bad times. There is no life of even a single
person which is without bad times. But, how
you choose to take those bad times is up to
you. Isn't it?"

"I suppose so," I said.

"Everyone has medical operations once in
a while. When you are going in for an
operation you know that you are doing it to
become better. There is something which
needs to be changed. There is something

which needs to be got rid of or cut out from your body so that it does not harm the rest of it. And you also know that there will be pain. However, you do have a choice. Knowing that you are going to have the pain, do you want to go through the period complaining, cribbing all the time that the pain is too much, knowing very well that you are doing it for your own good and that the pain is there so that you can be better? Or do you want to keep the goal in sight, that you are doing it to make yourself better, you are doing it to save something else, and that the pain is a consequence of your decision for a certain result?

"You see, in either case the pain is there but the choice is yours. Bad things happen to all of us. But, do we take them as lessons to be learnt or do we just go through them complaining as to why we are the ones who always have to face such bad times? The choice is always ours!"

"But why do we go through bad times at all?"

"A diamond, Cathy, is just a dirty stone under the earth. But, for its full brilliance, its power and beauty to shine through, it needs to be ground. It needs to be polished. And this is done by grinding it against another rough surface. Through the resulting friction, the same dirty stone becomes a beautiful, lustrous diamond. Essentially, it is the same with all of us."

"So bad things are meant to make us better?" I asked.

"Yes, every small thing, every small incident, every person we meet, every day we live, is meant to teach us, to polish us just a little bit more. All these lessons are necessary for us to learn and that is why such things happen in our lives.

"We must live in this awareness. Use every incident, use every person to learn from. And that would be fulfilling the purpose of your life. Don't let bad times grind you down, instead, let the bad times polish you up. The choice is yours."

"But passing through such a long life with bad times is extremely difficult. How does one make it easier?"

"As you pass through life, keep in mind that the attitude you carry with you is your most important friend. You can always depend on it and it will bring you in touch with people and circumstances which will take you higher. Do not maintain a pessimistic, bad attitude as you live your life because then it will attract towards itself things which are like it—pessimistic people, people with closed minds, people who complain often, people who discourage you a lot and times when you will feel nothing is going right. All these will be attracted towards you if you live with a pessimistic attitude.

"Conversely, if you live with an optimistic attitude, and are cheerful as you pass through life and its incidents and their lessons, you will pull towards yourself people who will encourage you, who will help you to grow, who will teach you things you do not know, who will expand your vision, and open your mind, people who will be cheerful themselves. How your life will turn out depends on your attitude. And your attitude depends on the choices you make. Everything around you is of your own making. It is your own creation. You are responsible for everyone and everything in your life, one way or another, whether you see it or not.

"Remember this, like attracts like! An eagle lives with eagles only. An eagle does not live with pigeons. It goes to hunt the pigeons. But it does not go and live with them. It does not mate with pigeons. Like attracts like!

"The attitude that you keep with you as your friend is your choice, and the choice has to be made at every moment till it becomes natural, till it becomes a habit."

"How do you make a habit of your attitude?" I asked.

"Do you know how habits are formed? They start out as one small innocent action on your part, something you want to try, something you want to explore. But that does

not make it a habit. It is the repetition of that
one-time action that does. When you try it
again and again and again, it becomes a habit
and a habit is a very strong thing. A good
habit is strong but a bad habit is strong too.
One in a positive way, the other in a negative
way. It is the same with your attitude. The
choice is open to you every minute. Let us
suppose that something bad happens in your
life. At that particular time, you have a
choice: 'How do I want to look at this that is
happening to me? Do I want to learn
something from it? Do I want to accept that it
is for my own good? That it is necessary for
me to grow? Or should I take it the other way
around?

"If you make the optimistic, the cheerful
choice, and do it again and again at every
instant, soon, before you realise it, it will
become a habit for you. You will become
addicted to your own cheerfulness, to your
positive attitude, to your positive mental
outlook in life. And once you become like
that, people will see you as such and feel
attracted towards you. These people will be
those who are also in need of growth, people
who are growing themselves, people who have
open minds.

"Once I met a great businessman of your
country and I asked him, 'What is the secret
of your success?'

"He told me, 'Suraj, I have a three-point formula for success.'

"I said, 'Will you share it with me?'

"He said, 'The three points are practice, practice and practice.'

"Practice makes perfect. The first time when something bad happens to you and you choose a positive outlook, it will be difficult. The next time you choose it, it is just a little bit easier. The third time you choose it, it is just little bit easier than the second time, and every time it keeps on becoming easier."

"So that is the way to create a positive outlook," I said.

"Yes, and one day, it will become difficult for you to choose a negative outlook. You will be so happy with the positive outlook as your friend that it will be difficult for you to give up that friend and choose a negative attitude. You will be unable to do it. Can you imagine that state?"

"So, practise, practise and practise. It is essential for your spiritual growth. And, do you know what will happen when you start choosing the positive outlook? The situations that you are in will not change initially. But, because you have changed, even situations where you have lessons to learn will start to change for you. They will not come in your life as much. People who discourage you will not come in your life as much as before. People who discourage you come in your life for your response to their discouragement. They feel happy when they succeed at their task of discouraging you. But when they try two or three times to do so and are unable to succeed, they go somewhere else. Nobody likes to fail. Neither do they. They want to succeed in their task of discouragement, and when they can't succeed with you, they will go and find somebody else. It is that simple.

"Soon you will see that situations, circumstances and people around you will change too. But, first let everything remain the same around you for now. You change first."

"So the responsibility is mine, like you said earlier."

"Yes, and remember that permanent change, long-lasting change will always be from the inside out. It will never be from outside in. One day, my master said to me, 'Suraj, my son, in the small time that we have on this earth to enlighten ourselves, to expand our vision, it is futile to go around trying to carpet the world. Instead, put on a pair of slippers yourself and walk the world as it is. You will save time and you will be able to move around. Instead of trying to change millions of people, change yourself first.'

"That's what he told me and I have never forgotten it, Cathy. It is easier and wiser to put on a pair of slippers yourself than to go around trying to carpet the whole world. Change yourself first. Everything around you will change as a result of what you have done, as a result of the decision you have taken. Don't try to change the whole world to suit you, change yourself first to create change in the external world."

"You certainly seem to have had interesting teachers, Suraj," I said.

"Yes, I have. One of my teachers in life, in fact, was Bruce Lee, a most unlikely spiritual teacher, don't you think?"

"The famous martial artist?"

"Yes, Cathy, the one and the same."

"I didn't know you knew him. What did he teach you? Did he teach you how to fight?"

"Well, I never met him. But, yes, he did teach me. And, apart from teaching me how to fight, he also taught me a lot about life."

"What did he teach you about life?" I asked.

"One of his lessons I carry with me always. A simple phrase, but it can change your life. He taught me, 'Take the best and discard the rest.'

"Bruce Lee was a very proficient martial artist and also a very evolved soul. You see, he was aware that in the world people fix themselves into moulds. People fix themselves into ideas. I am this, or I am that. This is like this or that is like that.

Christianity is so and so and Buddhism is like that. Hinduism is this and Islam is that and just because we are born into one or the other block, into one or the other fixed idea, we close our eyes to whatever is around us which may actually have the potential to teach us a lot. He recognised all this. And, he completely broke down the barriers between all of these differences.

"He said, 'Be open. What are you scared of? Be open, go and explore. Go and learn from everything that has the possibility to teach you. But keep your sense of direction. Don't go astray. Your direction, your focus must be one-pointed. Keep your mind open to learn from whatever has the possibility to teach you, and in everything, take the best and discard the rest.' This is just one of his lessons I have never forgotten."

"So one must be open to all directions?"

"Yes! You must follow this on a daily basis. It is not difficult. Morning to night, whatever happens to you has the possibility to teach you. Learn the lessons from things that happen to you, from instances which come in your life.

"Remember, all the people who come in your life have some lesson to give you, even children. Children have so much to teach us. It is we who are closed, Cathy. We should have the mind to understand and the eyes to see what they are trying to teach us. We should have a heart open to their wisdom, and then they become our teachers too."

> *Choosing the attitude you wish to adopt will probably be your most important decision!*

8

TEACHERS, TEACHERS EVERYWHERE

"I will tell you a small story. In Hindu mythology, one of the most famous seers is called Dattatreya. One day when Dattatreya was still a child, a king happened to visit the place where he lived. As the king saw the boy from a distance, he was amazed because this boy was absolutely shining, he was radiant, he was so cheerful, so happy, so enthusiastic. The king, even looking at him from a distance, knew that the boy lived in inner peace and inner joy. The king became eager to know how the boy had attained so much inner peace at such a young age. He went up to the boy and said, 'Can I ask you a question?'

"The boy replied, 'Yes.'

"The king asked him, "My son, you are so young and still you seem to live in some inner peace, in some inner joy, in some great understanding which we adults run after, strive after. Tell me, who is your teacher? Who has taught you so much?'

"The boy looked up at the king and said, 'I have many teachers. I learn from all of them.'

"The king was surprised. He said, 'But there must be one teacher whom you follow.'

"The boy replied, 'No, I learn from everything. Everything is my teacher.'

"And when he saw that the king wanted to know more, the boy explained, 'The earth is my first teacher. She teaches me to love in my heart those who hurt me, just as she does herself, and to give them the best that I have, just as she does herself.

" 'Water is my second teacher. Water gives life to whoever drinks it and it cleans whatever it touches and if it stops flowing, it stagnates.

" 'My third teacher is fire. Whatever fire burns, it purifies. It gives back to the original source. It gives warmth and it gives light. And while looking at fire and learning from it, I remember that I must absorb everything that life gives to me and learn from it, purify it, and give it back to its original source. I learn that I must light the way for others. I must give warmth and I must give light.

" 'My fourth teacher is the wind. The wind caresses the flowers and the thorns, both. It does not get attached to either of them. From the wind, I have learnt that friends and enemies are both to be touched. Neither should be got attached to.'

"The king was amazed. So much wisdom from such a small boy's mouth! On that morning, when the king had left for a ride on his horse, he had least imagined that his day was going to turn out like this. That he was going to learn so much from such an unlikely source.

"This king is now eager for more. His ears are open, his mind is open, his eyes are open and most of all, his heart is open. He wants to know more, he is eager to learn. So he asks the boy, 'Tell me more, tell me who is your fifth teacher.'

" 'My fifth teacher,' the boy says, 'is space. Just as the space accommodates the sun, moon and the stars and yet remains boundless itself, I have learnt that I must embrace all and yet remain unaffected by any of it.

" 'My sixth teacher is the moon. It waxes and it wanes and yet its essence remains the same. While watching the moon, I learnt that rising and falling, pleasure and pain, loss and gain, are simply just phases of life. They will pass away and while passing through these phases, I remain aware of who I am.

" 'My seventh teacher is the bright sun. The sun draws water from everywhere, and transforms it into clouds and returns it to the earth as rain. From the sun, I have learnt that I must gather knowledge from everywhere and transform it into practical wisdom that I can use and then I must share it with everybody, I must give it to everybody.

" 'My eighth master is a pigeon that was caught in a hunter's net. Hearing her cries, her friends tried to rescue her, but they got caught in the net also. From this, I have learnt that any reaction on my part, which is born out of attachment or out of emotion, is a trap for me. I always think twice before acting on a shallow emotion.

" 'My ninth teacher is the python. Once the python catches and eats its prey, it doesn't run after food again for a long, long time. The python has taught me to be satisfied once my needs are met, rather than making myself miserable running after things all the time.

" 'My tenth guru, my tenth master, is the ocean, where all the waters collect. Rivers and streams flow into it and rains fall on it. Yet, it never exceeds its boundaries. The ocean has taught me that no matter where I go in life, no matter what I go through, no matter how many bad incidents and kicks and blows I receive from life, I must remain unaffected and self-contained within myself.

" 'My eleventh teacher, O king, is the moth. The moth is drawn by light and he flies from his home to sacrifice himself in the flames. He gets burnt and he dies. I have learnt from him that once I see the dawn, once I see the light, even if it is only a hint of the light at a distance, I must overcome my fear and run at full speed to plunge myself into the transforming light of knowledge.

" 'My twelfth teacher is a bumblebee. The bumblebee, even before it takes the tiniest bit of nectar from a flower, hums and dances creating an atmosphere of joy around the flower. She gives more than she receives because while she takes the nectar, she also pollinates, and she ensures that there will be flowers for the seasons to come. I learnt from this that I must take only a little from nature to be cheerful and to enrich rather than destroy the life that sustains me, that keeps me alive.

" 'Go on please,' the king urges the boy.

" 'My thirteenth teacher is the honeybee. The honeybee gathers nectar from different blossoms, transforms it into honey and stores it in the hive for others to share. I also gather my teachings from every discipline and process the knowledge that I gain from all. I apply this knowledge to make me grow and I am ready to share this with anyone who wants it.

" 'My fourteenth teacher is the wild elephant. One day, a trapper took a female elephant in the mating season to the forest. The wild elephant in the jungle sensed her presence, ran from cover and fell into a pit that had been cleverly covered with branches and leaves. So, he was trapped. This elephant was tamed for the use of others. This has taught me, O king, to control my passions and my desires. All the worldly gifts, charms and temptations touch my senses and while chasing after these sensory pleasures, the powerful mind that I have is trapped and becomes a slave.

" 'Now, my fifteenth teacher. Do you want to know who my fifteenth teacher is?' "

" 'Yes, please continue,' the king replied.

" 'Okay. My fifteenth teacher is the deer. The deer has a keen sense of hearing and responds to sound instantly and with intelligence. He knows one sound from another, a good sound from a bad one, right from wrong, and although the deer is wary of noise, it becomes hypnotised when it hears the melody of the hunter's flute. I too keep my ears perked but I am often sceptical about what I hear. I have realised that all of us become spellbound by certain words, which, due to our desires and wants, we wait to hear. This trait causes misery in our lives and the lives of others. I have learnt this from the deer.

" 'My sixteenth teacher is the fish, which swallowed a baited hook and was caught and killed. This world, to me, is like a baited hook. As long as I remember the fish, I remain free of this hook and of the world.

" 'My seventeenth guru is the court dancer. She neither loves her customers nor expects them to love her. Yet, she waits for them and acts out a drama of love when they come. Neither the artificial love that she acts out nor the payment that she receives for it truly satisfies her, and so, I have realised that all human beings are like her. The world is enjoying us all and what it gives to us is too little for us to be satisfied with it. I have learnt to live with dignity and with self-respect without expecting any kind of fulfilment from this world. I have understood that the only fulfilment and peace I shall find is inside myself.

" 'My eighteenth teacher is a little bird which caught a worm and flew away. Larger birds pursued her and pecked at her, stopping only when this little bird dropped the worm. From this, I have learnt that the secret of survival is in renunciation, to give up, to let go, and not in possession, to want and to hold.

" 'My nineteenth teacher is the hungry baby who cries until he has the milk he needs. When he is full, the baby stops crying and sucking, and will not take any more milk. From this, I have learnt to remain joyful and to demand only when I need something truly.

" 'Are you bored, O king? Or do you want me to carry on?'

" 'Bored? I am totally engrossed in what you are saying, child. Please carry on.'

" 'One day, when I was begging for food, I met my twentieth teacher, a young woman. She told me to wait outside her door while she prepared the meal, and as she began cooking, her bangles jangled. She took one of them off, but the noise continued. Slowly, one by one, she took off all her bangles until only one remained, and when only one remained, there was silence. From this I learnt that wherever there is a crowd, there is a lot of noise and disagreement, and when there is only one, there comes peace and solitude and silence.

" 'My twenty-first teacher is the snake. It does not make a home for itself. But as it goes along, it stays in the holes of other creatures that have been abandoned. All it does is curve up inside the hollow of a tree for some time and then it carries on. The snake has taught me to adjust myself to my environment and to enjoy the resources that nature provides without building a permanent structure for myself anywhere. While I am floating through this life, I find plenty of places to rest and once I am rested, I move on. I don't get stuck anywhere.

" 'My twenty-second teacher is the arrow-maker. The arrow-maker gets so absorbed in sharpening his arrow-heads, that one day, the king and his entire army passed by without diverting his attention from his work.

I too have learnt to absorb myself in every task which comes in front of me, no matter how big or how small it may be. The more one-pointed my focus becomes, the greater my absorption in the task I am doing, and the greater my absorption in the task, the higher my awareness becomes. As my awareness becomes higher, my understanding about life grows.

" 'My twenty-third teacher is a little spider which wove herself a very cosy web. When a bigger spider came after her, she ran for the security of her web. But in fear she ran so fast that she got entangled in her own web, and the spider caught her and ate her. From this, I realised that we all try to make a secure future for ourselves. But, as we race along this life, we get so entangled in the daily routines and mundane things, that we forget that true safety does not lie in complicated planning or always worrying about the future, but in one-pointed awareness and absorption in the present moment.

" 'My twenty-fourth teacher is a small worm. One day, a bird caught this worm and placed it in its nest to eat later. When the bird began to sing, the worm got so caught up in the music, it began enjoying the music so much, that it forgot the danger it was in. From him, I learnt that, when we face death, if we too can develop the art of listening and become absorbed in the eternal sound of the universe, we shall forget about death and pass through it unaware and without fear.

" 'These are just some of my teachers, king.'

" 'Amazing,' the king said. 'Please tell me more.'

" 'I have learnt from all these and many others that the whole world is a school— teachings are found in everything and are everywhere. We can learn something from everything we see or from anyone who crosses our path, provided we have developed the qualities of a true student. We must have keen interest in knowledge. We must have an attitude of openness, an open heart and an open mind and we must have a strong determination to learn what is useful and to ignore and discard the rest. You know very well, O king, that a student's preparedness is inseparable from the teacher's willingness to open up. If a student is prepared to learn, a teacher expresses his ability to teach. This is not a secret, O king! This is one of the principles of learning,' Dattatreya ended.

"That was the day the king finally understood what real learning means and how one can learn from each and every small thing that happens in one's life. This lesson came to him from the small boy, Dattatreya. He realised that the true purpose of life is our own evolution, of the mind and of the spirit.

This life we are given is a learning process in itself. Our duty here, in the time that we have, is to learn from everything, everywhere, all the time, and to use all this knowledge for our growth," Suraj added.

> *An attitude is something you use to filter everything that happens to you!*

9

A GLASS OF WATER

For some time now, Suraj had been
expressing a desire to meet Nick, my
husband. He had not told me directly he
wanted to meet him, but he had been asking
questions about him frequently. What kind of
a person was he? What were his motivations?
What were his interests? He wanted to know
the details about my relationship with him.
How had we met? How had we decided to
spend our lives together? How had we got
married? Did either of us have very close
friends? It was almost as if he was sifting
through my mind and memory and trying to
put himself in exactly the position I was in
now. It was as if he wanted to know
everything that I knew so that he could see
my relationship from my eyes, from my point
of view.

On the other hand, Nick had generally
been ignoring the topic of Suraj since the day
I had discussed him. He had been keeping to
himself for the past few days. Like I said

earlier, it was as if we were living under the same roof, two people together and yet far away. He would keep busy with himself, involved in his work or his activities at home like watching television, reading magazines, calling his friends, or once in a while even going out without telling me where he was going.

And I too had taken to being by myself while at home. I had a lot to think about. My meetings with Suraj and the things he had been telling me had turned my life upside down. His way of looking at things and his way of accepting life were completely alien to me. Growing up in this most advanced of countries, I had become a person who was motivated by material riches, possessing a good house, a good partner, a good family. Having plenty of money in the bank, judging people by how they appeared and how well their career was doing were my priorities. So after Suraj came into my life, it was as if my whole value structure had broken down. In fact that is exactly what Suraj was asking me to do—change my whole value structure—everything I had learnt so far about values, about the world, how to judge it, how to relate to the world, and how to relate with people. He was asking me to give that up completely and to substitute it with a new value structure.

I could not deny the fact that, even though it was very difficult for me, what he was telling me was true. For example, one day, he pointed out that my present value structure was not conducive to my growth. The value structure which he wanted me to adopt would in fact gear everything that happened to me in my life, or every person I met, towards helping me to grow more. I could not deny the truth in that. He told me that in my present way of living, it was as if I was judging books by their cover, and he was right. Because that is what I had been doing, judging people by their external appearance. I was striving for material possessions as the end goals of my life. And much as I didn't like accepting this, I had to. There was no other way.

We had spent many days together and he had spoken to me on many diverse topics and subjects. So one day, when I met him, I asked him, "Suraj, what exactly is it that you want me to understand? How exactly is it that you want me to change in my way of looking at things, in my outlook and in my attitude? What is it that you want me to do? Remember that story you told me about the king who wanted the gist of all the spiritual books in one sentence?"

"Yes, of course I do. These are things not to be just spoken and forgotten about. These are things to live by, so how is it possible for me to say it and forget it?"

"Okay, Suraj, then tell me in one sentence, in one line, what is it that you want me to change in my outlook? What is it that you are trying to teach me? Make it simple for me."

"I knew this was going to come up some day, Cathy. You are too smart to accept things as they are without trying to simplify them more. But, as it happens, I do have an answer for you, and here it is. In one sentence, what I want you to do as you pass through life, is to see the glass half full and not half empty," he replied smilingly.

"What? Is that the gist of all your philosophy of life? Is that the bottom-line of what you have been trying to tell me all these days?"

"Exactly, that is all there is to it. Everything will follow from this. If you do that at every moment of your life, Cathy, everything will be positive in your life. And if everything is positive in your life, there is no way God can be far away from you. There is no way you will not want to be close to God. Now imagine a glass half full of water. All the people in this world will look at it in one of two ways. Some will look at it and say it is half empty and some will look at it and say it is half full. On this crucial way of thinking, on this crucial choice that you make, whether it is half full or half empty, depends your entire life. If you choose the positive outlook, if you choose to think and feel that it is half full instead of half empty, you will think to yourself, 'At least I have half a glass of water. It is not as if I have nothing. So let me be thankful that I have a glass half full of water.' That is the positive way of looking at it, and when you look at it in a positive way and feel that you have something, you will always be thankful for it. Having this positive outlook will make you concentrate at any given moment on what you have rather than what you do not have. As the Lord Buddha told us, 'You are what you think all the time.' "

"He said we are our thoughts?" I asked.

"No, Cathy. He said our thoughts make up what we are, what we think about all the time, we become. Now, if you always think positive thoughts, you will become a positive person, you will have a positive character, you will be a happy and cheerful person. Anger will slowly diminish in your life. You will not have the time or the energy to carry grudges and feelings of hate inside you. Slowly you will develop a personality which will attract to itself people, things and circumstances which are also positive and which will help you to progress faster in your chosen direction."

"And then?"

"Then, life, instead of becoming a drudgery for you, will become a pleasant journey. You will go through it and enjoy it so much that you will give love to people and you will receive their love. You will have a good, strong and healthy relationship with your husband, with your children, with your friends, with your parents and with society. Nothing will have the capacity to get you down.

"If you use everything for your growth, people will seek you for advice. You will always be looking at what you have, what you have received and because of this you will be thankful. You will start having an attitude of gratitude towards God and the universe and that will take you even higher.

"Eventually, Cathy, will come a stage when you will realise that everything is given to you from God in love. Once you come to this stage, you will realise that you have no role to play at all. You have done nothing to deserve all that has been given to you. It is as if a father in love has given so much to the child and the child feels that it has done much work to deserve it all. It is not so, and you will come to realise this at that stage.

"And, when you realise that God loves you, he gives you everything that you need, he is everything and you are nothing, you completely dissolve the 'I' that you are carrying inside you. 'I' am this, 'I' am that, 'I' have done this, 'I' have done that, 'I' should do this, 'I' should deserve this, 'I' can do this, 'I' want this. That 'I' will dissolve completely and when that dissolves, Cathy, you will see the miracle of this life. Once you get yourself out of the picture, God will come into you. Once you empty yourself out from this container, God will fill it.

"Then, you will still be you, but you will not be you. You will be full of God. God will be in you and you will be in God. He and you will be as one in this body of Cathy.

"Everything that you speak, everything that you do, everything that you desire, will all come from God. It will be as if God is speaking, God is saying, God is listening, God is desiring.

"That is the miracle, and it is possible. And this tremendous, overwhelming miracle depends, right now in this moment, on how you choose to live the rest of your life. You see, it is that simple. Every moment is a choice. Make this choice right now and continue to make it at every moment. That is the basic rule of life.

"This journey may take you a lifetime, it may take you ten lifetimes or it may take you just half a lifetime. The desire that you carry with you, the enthusiasm that you carry with you, the focus, the single-mindedness and the determination, these make up your speed. These decide the time that it will take you to reach your destination.

"As the Chinese say, 'Even a thousand-mile journey begins with a single step.' So, take the first step. Let us take it together. That is why I am here. To take the first few steps with you because after that we must all walk by ourselves. Let us take the first step now and look to the end of the journey. Let us keep our eyes on the goal and walk boldly with full faith that we are walking towards God. In fact, God is accompanying us towards Himself and He shall push us every time we stop. He shall support us when we are tired. He shall hold us up when we stumble and fall. And, He shall guide us when we lose our way. There is no downside to this journey. There is no negative side to this decision that you make. Even though it may sometimes seem like this to you, there is no downside. There is nothing wrong that can happen. The only variable factor once you have decided and taken the first step on this journey is the amount of time that it may take you to reach the end. But, keep your eyes on the goal and you will not have any obstacles.

"One of your fellow countrymen, a great businessman, one day told me, 'You know, Suraj, I have realised after twenty years of working in companies and managing people and affairs, that obstacles and problems are what happen to you when you take your eyes off the final goal.' He said, 'As long as my eyes are on the final goal, I don't see what comes before me, I just keep walking, I know where I am going, I just keep going step by step, and everything that comes in my way, I take it in my stride and overcome it or I walk around it. But the moment I take my eyes off the goal and start looking at the things which come in my way, that is when all the problems seem to happen to me. And eventually, I start giving so much time to the problems that I create more and more of them because it is true that whatever we give our attention to becomes true in our lives. If we are always thinking of lack—I lack this, I lack that—sure enough we develop that lack in our lives. If we give our thoughts, time and mind to positive feelings about what we have, what we have received, sure enough we receive those things. So, when I start giving my time to those problems, Suraj, I create more problems.

"Now, Cathy, that is a very powerful bit of wisdom from a businessman and it is applicable not only to business, but to all aspects of our life, including the spiritual.

"So, let us take a decision right now. Are you ready?

"Be bold!

"Be brave!

"Be strong!

"Be bold, stand up and take a decision in your heart—this is the way you are going to live, and then leave everything to Him. Have faith that He shall guide you, and He will."

> *To change your life,*
> *see the glass half full,*
> *not half empty!*

10

JUST BREATHING

Since the first day that Suraj had asked me to greet the sun and God in the morning and ask for energy, I had been doing it regularly. He told me that this was to be one of the few basic exercises which would prepare me to perceive more, to remove certain blocks and to hasten the flow, which would make me more open to new concepts and lead to a rise in my level of consciousness.

Every morning I faithfully greeted the sun and God and asked them for life-giving energy which I could turn into positive, spiritual-growth experiences. As the days went by, I was noticing a subtle change in the regular procedure I had been following.

I remember the first day when I woke up and walked out to greet the sun. I remember how I felt when I did it. I was doing it in a state of complete non-believing, I had no faith in anything I was saying. The words came out of my mouth with hesitation and I truly did

not expect to get any result from that
exercise. Now, I had begun to actually look
forward in the morning to receiving the sun's
first rays, lifting my hands up in the air,
standing with my face turned up towards the
sky and greeting the sun and God. I had
started looking forward to telling them that I
am here, I am here waiting for energy, and
asking for help to turn this energy into
positive experiences so that I may grow, so
that I may become more complete, so that I
may become happier, so that I may be closer
to them.

Now, I could feel the sun's rays touching
my body, touching my face, heating up my
eyes and my skin. I could feel a certain subtle
transmission taking place as the rays seeped
into my skin. I could actually feel that I was
drawing energy from the sun.

That brought me to another realisation—
that all these years of my life I had never
really understood how much energy the sun
exuded. I had never understood how much
the sun was giving us. I had never realised
how all life depends on the energy received
from the sun. All these things, I was just
beginning to understand.

And, I was also developing a feeling of
gratitude, of appreciation towards what was
happening to me. I felt thankful for Suraj
coming into my life, for whatever reasons. I
felt thankful for the way my life had changed

direction after I had met him. I felt thankful
to God for the way my thinking was being
altered, for the way my value system was
being changed and the way I was beginning to
understand certain deeper truths of existence
and of peoples' behaviour.

Suraj also taught me another exercise
which he said was one of the most basic and
necessary to gain control over our minds. One
day, he explained to me the importance of the
breath, how the breath had a direct
correlation with the working of the mind.

He started off by telling me, "Cathy, for a
minute, step back from your mind and look at
it. Just observe it for a minute. What does
your mind do? It jumps from one thought to
another. It cannot stand still, it has to have
something to play on. Either it is here or it is
there. One moment it is with you, you are
thinking of what you want to do. The next
moment it is with your friend who is at home,
and you are thinking of what she must be
doing. The next moment it is with your
brother in some other part of the country. The
next moment it is with your husband. The
next moment it is with your past and the next
moment it is with your future. The mind
cannot stand still. You see, Cathy, the mind
is like an inexhaustible worker. But, it does
not have the capability, because it is not used
to it, of being still. It can do all the work you

give it. But, if you ask it to sit still, it cannot do so. It keeps asking you for more work and if you don't give it anything to do, it goes and finds something to spend time on.

"It is like a drunken monkey. Now, you know how fickle a monkey is. One moment he is doing this, the next moment he is doing that. He is touching this, he is touching that. He cannot be still. And, imagine if the monkey is drunk. What will he be like? All his traits of restlessness, impatience and curiosity will be doubled. That is what your mind is like, Cathy. You have to bring this mind under control and it is a very difficult thing to do. How do you even start doing it? When the task is so huge, how do you start?"

"How do you start?" I asked, repeating his words.

"The secret to that, Cathy, is breath. The breath is probably the most important thing in life because, as we believe, we have life only from the moment we start breathing to the moment your breath leaves your body. Then you are declared dead. So, from the moment you start breathing, you become alive and the moment you stop breathing, you die. And, through all these years of existence between your first inhalation, that is birth, and the last exhalation, that is death, the only thing which remains constant is that you are breathing every moment of your existence. You don't sleep as much, you don't eat as much, you don't think as much. But, yes, you breathe all the time. Even when you sleep, you breathe. Even when you are unconscious, you are breathing. Breath is the secret to life.

"In India, the ancient yogis, who were actually just scientists experimenting on human behaviour and consciousness, found that when the mind is in an accelerated state, the breath accelerates and when it is in a calm state, the breath becomes deep and calm. So, as a logical next step, they said, 'If there is a correlation between the two, can we then not try and control the breath and as a result of controlling the breath, control the mind?'

"They tried this, Cathy, and it worked. These ancient yogis in India, really, who were they? They were people who were contemplating, who were experimenting with heightened states of consciousness. Basically they were conducting experiments on the human mind, the human body, the human spirit, and on human consciousness. That is what they did for thousands of years. They charted out an inner map for us.

"The entire growth in the Orient, so far, till this age, has been towards the inner life of the human being, whereas in the West, it has always been towards the outer life of the human being. People in the West are tuned to seek happiness externally. They want to go out and buy material things and have the best utilities. They want to have the best of every external thing in this world. And they feel that this will eventually lead them to inner happiness—that if they have enough they will be happy.

"In the East, the trend has been completely the opposite. People there understood early on in life that external possessions or belongings cannot give one inner peace because whatever one may have on the outside, emotions like anger, hurt, feeling bad, depresssion, the feel of your ego, your pride and anger don't change. So, they tried another approach and said, 'Let us go inside ourselves first and try to make ourselves happy from the inside out. In that case if we achieve happiness in our inner lives, then it doesn't matter what we have outside. We shall always be happy, irrespective and regardless of our external circumstances.'"

"Is that the correct approach, then?" I asked.

"There is good and bad to both these approaches, Cathy. You can see that the West has developed differently from the East. It is because thousands of years ago they made two different choices. They each made a choice and as their actions led from one to the other based on their first initial choice, two completely different lifestyles developed. And as two completely different lifestyles developed, two completely different societies came into being. But we are getting off the track here. Let us get back to the breath."

"We always seem to go off track, don't we, Suraj?"

"Never for long," he smiled. "Anyway, the ancient masters found that by controlling the breath, one can actually control the speed and processes of one's mind.

"Cathy, I want you to learn a very simple way of breathing, called 'diaphragmatic breathing'. In simple words, instead of using your lungs to breathe, as we have learnt to do so far, you use your diaphragm to breath. I shall teach you the technique. It is extremely simple. Even a child can learn it. All it takes is two minutes. But just because it is simple, don't discount its effectiveness or its importance.

"Generally in life you will find that the most profound pieces of wisdoms are the simplest. The most fantastic of occurrences are in fact very simple processes. They follow very simple laws."

Saying this, Suraj taught me the technique of diaphragmatic breathing. He explained how in this hectic and fast-paced world, we have learnt to breathe shallowly from our chest. He said that while breathing as we do now, we use about 30 per cent of our lung

capacity for breathing. The remaining 70 per
cent remains unused or full of stagnant, stale
air, which should actually be expended.

"Instead of pulling the air into your lungs,
pull it down into your stomach. Let your
stomach expand as you inhale through your
nose," he told me. He said that the diaphragm
is situated below the lungs and above the
belly and when we try and fill this part of our
body with air, we use 75 to 80 per cent of our
lung capacity. As a result of that, the
inhalation and exhalation of the air cleanses
80 per cent of your lung capacity which in
itself gives you a lot more energy and at the
same time a lot more purification is taking
place with every exhalation.

"Do you recall ever getting angry, Cathy?
Getting angry at someone or just feeling so
frustrated that you wanted to hit out at
something? Or getting into a fight with
anybody suddenly? Under these circumstances we happen to puff up our chest and
we start breathing more shallowly. The
breath comes into the chest, and the chest
expands. The breath is let out and the chest
deflates. Now take a completely opposite case
when you are asleep, you are fully relaxed,
no worries on your mind, your consciousness
is in some other state. Your body
automatically starts breathing from
your diaphragm, from your belly. This
technique is also called belly breathing in

various cultures. In an extreme state of relaxation, your body takes long, deep inhalations, holds for some time and exhales, as opposed to a state where you are very aggressive, perturbed or disturbed. In that case, your body breathes very shallowly, holds for very little time and exhales immediately. Just by controlling your breath, you can have more control over your mind. When your mind is disturbed, if you consciously start doing diaphragmatic, deep-belly breathing, you will see that in a few moments your mind will quieten down. It calms down."

He sat down in front of me and demonstrated this method of belly breathing. And he made me repeat slowly every step of it till he felt I was doing it correctly.

"Start out with doing this five minutes in the day as you get up and five minutes at night before you go to sleep. And slowly, if possible, try and increase the time. The final goal, Cathy, is to do this on a regular basis all the time. Right now, your body carries on breathing shallowly and you will start out by using diaphragmatic, deep-belly breathing as a tool for when you want to slow down your thoughts or control your emotions. Eventually, I want you to reach a stage where diaphragmatic breathing will be a regular function of your body. From morning to night, you shall breathe like that. At that time, you can use shallow breathing as a tool, if you ever come across circumstances in which you want to aggravate your mind, accelerate its working or heighten your emotions. See, I am trying to turn the breathing pattern completely around. And it is not difficult to do so because actually the natural rhythm of your body, its natural breathing pattern is what I am trying to teach you again. Your body does it instinctively when you are away, when your consciousness is away from your body, when you sleep. But when your consciousness associates with your body, worldly things, emotions and worldly inputs, your body changes its breathing pattern to adapt to all the other connections that you have made in your consciousness. It is not so difficult to turn it around but obviously effort must be put in from your side."

"Obviously," I answered.

After all, with an unconventional teacher like this, I had to try and be an unconventional model student myself.

> *Just because a path or wisdom*
> *is simple, do not discount its*
> *effectiveness or value !*

11

CHOOSING, ACTING, CHANGING

"As I said earlier, through life, the greatest friend, the greatest support, that you can have is your own attitude. And on this depends everything that comes into your life—how everything is accepted and how it is utilised to make you grow.

"You are going to go through life one way or another. In that you don't have a choice. You are going to grow. In that also, you don't have a choice. But how fast you grow and how smoothly you grow, in this you do have a choice, and the choice depends on the attitude you use to look at or to receive the things that come into your life. An attitude is something you use to filter everything that happens to you.

"Incidents, people, happenings, events— all of these are in a way neutral. Without your attitude to filter them, they are neither good nor bad. But depending on your attitude, they can be perceived as either good or bad.

"You have a choice, as I explained to you earlier. Do you want to see the glass half full, or do you want to see the glass half empty? The choice between having a positive attitude, being an optimist and trusting, or having a negative attitude, being a pessimist and fearful, is up to you. And you have to pick one as your partner in life."

"We have all heard so much about the benefits of having a positive mental attitude. And they are all true. Everything that comes to us in life has both good and bad. There is nothing or no one who is only good or only bad in life. There is a percentage of good and bad in everybody and everything. When we look at the rose, we accept the thorns, don't we? When you receive the sunshine, you accept the heat that comes along with it, don't you?"

"I've been doing a lot more of that recently," I smiled.

"So, do you want to go through life counting your blessings, Cathy, or would you rather go through life complaining about your problems? You see, one must understand that the important thing is what one is giving attention to all the time. If you have a positive mental attitude, you will obviously focus more on the things that you do have and not so much on the things that you don't have. In this case concentrating on the things that you do have, on your blessings, will give you more because you will attract more of the same towards you. That is the law of attraction that we spoke about earlier.

"And the same holds true for concentrating on your deficiencies, things which you don't have or your problems. The more you concentrate on them, the more you enlarge them, the more power you give to them.

"Do you remember the poem, 'I had the blues because I had no shoes, till down the street I met a man who had no feet?' This man was sad because he had lost his shoes and in that sadness he was walking down the street complaining and cribbing about it. And then he saw a man sitting there who did not have any feet. And seeing this crippled man, he realised that he was lucky for he had only lost his shoes and still had his feet. 'If I didn't have my feet, I would not even bother about the shoes. At least I am able to walk,' he thought.

"Don't forget that we attract to ourselves and literally become what we give our attention to. Where our thoughts are all the time, that's what we become. And I think it is time for a story now."

"That's what the Buddha said, didn't he?" I interrupted.

"Yes, he did. But now, the story.

"Once upon a time, in ancient India, there was a holy priest, who lived in a house by the road. And across the same road was the house of a prostitute, and both of them, the priest and the prostitute could see each other's houses. Now the priest was a very pious man. He had his schedule set from morning to night. He would get up early in the morning. He would meditate. He would take his bath. He would pray to God. He would go out for counselling and guiding people. He would help the needy. And that is how his whole day progressed till in the evening he would retire for the night and go to sleep.

"But, every morning when the priest would get up, he could hear the dancing and singing going on in the prostitute's house. And he could see people going in and out of her house, even early in the morning. He would to think to himself, 'I wonder what kind of a lady this is that she spends her whole life in sinful acts and does not find even a little bit of time to give her attention to God or to worry about her own growth. The whole day, she is singing for these men, she is dancing for them. She is sleeping with them, she is selling her body.' He would constantly think about these things. As evening would come, he would think, 'In half an hour now, the music is going to start and it is going to carry on till early tomorrow morning.' He would carry these thoughts with him unconsciously all the time."

"Then what happened?" I asked.

"Eventually, he finished his life, died, and went up to heaven. And when he got there, he met God who brought him in and gave him a tour of the whole place. After about half an hour there, God told him, 'Your time here is over and you cannot be in heaven anymore. You have to leave.' And with that God led him out.

"On his way out, the priest saw that the prostitute was sitting in heaven. He was shocked. He turned around and said, 'God, what are you doing? I have been your devotee for my whole life and this prostitute, she stayed across the road from me and I know what her life was. From morning to night, she would entertain men, sing for them, dance for them, she would sell her body. That is what she did the whole day for money and you are turning me out of heaven while she is sitting here. There has to be some mistake.'

"God turned around and told him, 'My son, there is no mistake. In your life, even while you were performing the role of a priest, your thoughts always dwelt on the actions of this prostitute. The whole day you were thinking about the dancing, the singing and the entertaining that she was doing and even though day after day you performed many rites and prayers, your thoughts were always on her actions. Now whatever merit you had accumulated has run out by your spending half an hour here. It is time for you to go.'

"The priest said, 'But how can she be here then? You know all that she has done? How can you allow her to remain here?'

"God said, 'Her place is here because even though her body was performing all of the actions, you told Me about, even though she was dancing and singing and entertaining these men, her mind was always on your actions. Just as you could see her house across the road, she could see yours too. And whenever she would get up in the morning, she would say to herself, Oh, what a pious man that priest is! He prays all the time to God, he helps the needy, he counsels and gives guidance to people. I should try and lead my life in that direction. Her awareness and her consciousness was always on the good deeds that you were doing. Therefore, by that merit, she has the right to be here.'

"The moral of this story, Cathy, is that whatever we give our attention, awareness and consciousness to whatever we think about all the time, that is what we tend to become, that is what we tend to attract in our lives.

"So, we come back again to attitude. You have a choice now, and at every moment, of how you want to live the rest of your life. Do you want to live looking at life from a positive attitude or a negative one? You have to decide and you have to follow your decision."

"Yes, I remember that. You told me the same thing earlier," I said.

"Remember also that all the knowledge in this world is no good to you until and unless you start putting it into action. Thinking and knowing don't change a person. It is in the action that the change occurs.

"For thousands of years, Cathy, there has been no dearth of knowledge in this world. There have been scriptures to guide human beings from the beginning of time. But how many through the centuries have really followed the teachings? Everybody reads these scriptures. Reading is the easy part—five minutes in the morning, five minutes in the evening. But that reading does not change you. If that reading plants a thought in your mind and if that thought is followed, if it is acted upon, that changes you. And the process of change starts with one small action and eventually it expands and expands and you realise that you are living your whole life in a different way."

"It's that Chinese saying again, isn't it, about the thousand-mile journey?" I said.

"Yes. So, make a choice now and decide to act upon it. Success in any venture, including the spiritual venture, comes to those who dare to act. It never goes to the ones who don't act. People have never been rewarded in life for what they knew. They have been rewarded only for what they did.

"Walk this path by choosing a mental attitude which is positive over a mental attitude which is negative, and you have nothing to lose. In fact, you have everything to gain. In any case, you are not going to be more miserable or unhappy than you are now. So, don't just sit back and think about it. Accept it. Try it out, adapt it to your life. Live it out. That is the secret."

"But how does one start?" I queried.

"Start slowly. Start having a positive attitude, first, in the small things of life, in small incidents. Try and make yourself happier slowly, one step at a time. A journey well begun is already half done. So start slowly and walk a step at a time. Any failures, or any setbacks that you come upon during your walk down the path can actually be turned into stepping stones if you have a positive mental attitude. But if you have a negative mental attitude, every small pebble that comes in your way will become a stumbling block that you feel you cannot overcome.

"The choice is in front of you now. And you must choose! Choose the way and the direction of your life now! Decide how you want to live each day, with what attitude you want to see it. Problems come for everybody and they will come for you too, but what attitude do you want to face them with? Do you want to be chained down by your negatives or do you want to fly on your positives?" Suraj said.

"Remember that all the problems you face in your lifetime have a lifetime of their own. They come, they stay a while, they go. They end. They have been sent your way to teach you something, to give you a lesson, something which will help you grow in life. So, learn from them willingly and learn from them well. Face your problems. Accept them, learn from them. Work through them and then bid them goodbye. Let them go, and do all this with a positive attitude.

"All the problems, mishaps and difficulties that come your way in your life will change you. That is what they are for: to cause change in you because you may be lacking in something. You have not learnt a particular lesson as yet or you may have been doing something incorrectly that needs to be corrected. Problems are given to you so you can take a step back and think about how you can do things better and how you can become

better. Think about why the problem has
come in the first place and then change what
needs to be changed." .

"So all problems come to change us?" I
asked.

"Yes, that one thing is for sure. That all
problems will change you in one way or
another. But the crucial factor is whether
they will make you a better person or a worse
person than you originally were. Will these
problems lift you higher or are they a weight
on your head which makes you stoop? Will
you step over them so that you may see
further or will you carry them on your head,
that you feel their weight all the time? That is
for you to decide," Suraj ended.

I returned home to find Nick waiting for me.

"How was your day with Suraj?" he asked.

"Pretty amazing, as usual," I replied.

"Exactly what is he? Is he a guru or a holy
man? You told me he is from India. Is he one
of those guys in orange robes and long hair?"

"He is none of those. But exactly what he
is, I myself can't describe," I answered.

"You have been spending so much time
with him, Cathy. What is happening?"

"Nothing is happening, Nick. We have
become very good friends, that's all. Actually,
we are more than friends because I feel it is
also a teacher-student relationship that we

share. I am learning a lot from him. But apart from that it is completely platonic."

"You told me he is twenty-nine years old. Now, it is not possible that you can have a platonic relationship with a young twenty-nine years old man, especially one with whom you are spending so much time," Nick said.

"Don't you think it is possible that two young people can just be good friends?" I asked.

"No, I don't think it is possible. Not if one is a male and the other is a female. I can't see how a completely platonic, deep relationship is possible between a male and a female. It just doesn't work like that," he retorted.

"I don't know what is going on in your mind, Nick. But, believe me. It is completely platonic. I'm telling you. And in fact, you should see for yourself. He wants to meet you. He has been asking me about you for the last few days. So why don't you just meet him and see for yourself—make your own judgements of what he is, what he says."

"I don't think I have any need for a guru in my life," he muttered.

"I am telling you that he is not a guru in the usual sense of the word. He is more of a teacher. He is very normal, just like you and me except that he lives his life on completely different principles and values. And he seems to know about everything a lot more deeply than we do. His motivations are completely different. His awareness about things is completely different from ours. His behaviour is completely different. When you meet him, Nick, you should ask him all these questions that you are asking me. He can tell you better about himself than I can describe him to you," I said.

"Yeah, if I meet him—and that's a big if—if and when I meet him, I will ask him, but right now I don't think that I have any need for somebody to come into my life and try to tell me how to live it."

"Nick, make your own decisions, but we are planning to go jet-skiing in a couple of days. Why don't you come along with us at that time?" I said.

"You are going jet-skiing with him now!" he shouted.

"Yeah," I tried to remain calm.

"And when did you say this will be?" he asked.

"We will go in the next couple of days. Why don't you try and come along with us at that time?" I replied.

"I'll think about it. But you just go ahead and do what you want. You want to go jet-skiing. Fine. You want to go away with him somewhere, you want to spend all your time with him. It is okay by me. It is your life after all. You have to be happy. You entered this relationship out of choice. So, you can make your own decisions about it too. Just go ahead and do whatever you want," Nick retorted angrily.

That was the end of the conversation for that night. We spent some time just sitting together, but separately, not conversing, and eventually we changed our clothes and retired for the night.

> *Thinking and knowing never changes a person. The change occurs only with action!*

12

A GLIMPSE OF SVNLIGHT

The next day, when I went to meet Suraj in his room, there was somebody else there with him. Another woman. Long, black hair, black eyes, quite fair, with a very delicate built, and I was to find out later that her name was Amy. I must admit that when I first saw her with Suraj, they seemed so much at ease with each other, so comfortable together that a feeling of jealousy went through me, and it surprised me too.

Amy was Suraj's friend from many years ago. Suraj had apparently come into her life also at a critical time and turned it around just as he was attempting to do with mine. Suraj introduced me to her and then they continued their conversation which was related, as it always was with Suraj, to God, happiness, success in life, etc.

"What are you both talking about?" I asked.

Amy smiled and replied, "He is telling me the correct way to go after a correct life."

"That's kind of confusing, isn't it?" I said.

"Not really," she replied, smiling once again.

"Cathy, tell me something," Suraj said. "Once you become aware that life is a lesson, that life is meant to teach us, to make us grow and for us to evolve, what is the correct way to live after that?"

"The correct way to live would be to become aware at every instant that everything is meant to make us grow, to learn from and with that attitude, to try and seek happiness in life. As far as I can reason or understand, Suraj, that would be the correct way," I replied.

"Now, according to what I was telling Amy, that would be something exactly not to do," he said.

"Why?" I asked.

"Because if you look for happiness or success as goals, or as aims of life and you chase after them, you are bound to be disappointed, Cathy. Both happiness and success in life are not goals by themselves. They cannot be achieved by rushing after them. Even rushing after them or trying all the time to find them will eventually become a hindrance for you in their achievement."

"Then what would be the correct way to live our lives according to you?"

"According to me, happiness is a by-product of a life well-lived. That is all. And I believe that if you live your life correctly and in the proper way, happiness in every field, and abundance, both material and spiritual, will come to you. The idea is, that we must treat everybody and everything as originating from God.

"Remember, I told you earlier, that to truly live, we must do. We must not only know, we must not only think, we must actually act, we must do. Living is in the doing. It is not in the knowing or the understanding. So, we must live every day treating everything that happens to us or every person around us as originating in God. And by living our life this way, by taking both the negative and the positive in a positive way as originating from God, we will achieve success and happiness and abundance in our life."

"I really don't see how that will happen, Suraj," I said.

"Remember what Jesus said? He told his followers not to worry about the things of the world or their desires for the things of the world. Jesus said, 'Seek ye first the kingdom of heaven and all else will be added on to you.' I believe Jesus meant that one should see God in every small instance in one's life, in every person around us and in this way to live, we gather all happiness and material pleasures along the way. And one more important thing. If we live our life this way, we will accept these pleasures in the correct way and not get carried away by them or get stuck in them. They will not affect our ego or our pride. When you take the pleasures and the pains of the world as originating in God, you will not get elevated or inflated by them. You will take them, enjoy them and let them go.

"I remember, long ago my master told me, 'Suraj, everything under this sky is yours. It is put there by God for his children to enjoy. But, remember that the critical word is enjoy. Do not get attached to them. Do not try to possess them, whether people, things or incidents. Enjoy everything. Life is meant to be fun, life is not meant to be a struggle. One has to flow through life. How can you flow through life if you are struggling at every step? Getting attached at every step? So, enjoy everything that your father gives you. But, do not try to possess any of it. Do not get attached to any of it. Do not get stuck in any of it.' "

With that, Suraj got up to leave and I got up with him. I thought we were all going to leave together.

"No, Cathy, I have to meet somebody alone for about two hours. Why don't you and Amy sit here in the room and wait for me? Feel free to order some room service if you wish," Suraj said.

"Okay," I replied.

On his way out, he turned around and asked me, "Did you ever feel the desire to have children, Cathy?"

It was typical of Suraj asking the strangest questions at the strangest times. Here, I was sitting in his room that he was leaving, leaving with me a lady I had just met and whom I knew nothing about, and he was loudly and openly asking me a very personal and private question in front of her.

How was I to reply?

"The thought did come into my mind a couple of times, Suraj," I answered reluctantly.

"Okay," he replied lightly, "we'll talk about that a little later. I have to go now. See you both later." And with that he left.

I turned around, smiled at Amy and waited for her to speak.

"He is truly amazing, isn't he?" she said.

"You bet. I don't think I have ever met anybody like him," I replied.

"How long have you known him?"

"Just a few weeks, as a matter of fact."

"And how long did he say he would be with you?" Amy asked.

"He mentioned nine and a half weeks when I first met him. Why, does it have any significance?"

"Well, you are lucky. Nine and a half weeks is a short amount of time in which to turn your life around. With me, it took much longer."

"You mean, he did the same thing with you?" I asked.

"Oh yes! I didn't know where my life was going, how I was living, for what I was living, when he came into my life. And, he was in and out of it for almost a year before I felt safe and secure enough, to be away from him for an extended period," Amy replied.

"Where are you from, Amy?" I asked.

"From Minnesota," she replied.

"Minnesota? The coldest state in the US and here we are in Florida—one of the hottest," I said.

"That is the thing with Suraj. One time he is in one part of the world, the next you know he is on the other side of the world. Occasionally, you hear that he is back in India but there nobody seems to know where he is. And wherever he is, I see him helping people. Mostly women, though sometimes he helps men too."

"Why does he help women more than men? What's the reason? Tell me more about him, Amy. It seems you know him much more closely than I do."

"You are probably right, Cathy," she replied. "I have known him for many years now, and every once in a while when I get stuck, I have to talk to him or I come to meet him as I am doing now, for a couple of days or

even for a few hours. It always works for me.
He is able to clarify my doubts and to show
me the light. But, once that is done, he starts
pushing me away. Once the knowledge is
given, it has to be lived and that is why Suraj
does not like anyone to get stuck to him or get
attached to him. He does not believe in
becoming a crutch for the people he helps. He
believes that eventually we all must help
ourselves. 'Knowledge is from God,' he says,
'and we, who are open to it or who have been
graced by it, have a duty and a responsibility
to pass it on to others.' But, once that is
done, each person must help himself. The
knowledge has to be lived out in this life and
in that no one can help you."

"Tell me more about him. Why do you
generally see him helping women more than
men?"

"I asked him that once, you know. His
answer was that in general women are at a
stage in the evolution of this planet where
they are more perceptible to the knowledge.
God knows what that means, Cathy. But, that
is what he said. And I believe, he also feels
that women are much more receptive to love,
in general, than men. And since all
knowledge comes from God, which is pure
love, and is given in love, and is meant to
create love, women take to it or accept it
easier than men. Which is not to say that men
are any less than women. But they have

different needs and they need to be taught in a different way. As far as I know, he has many men who are his disciples also and from different parts of the world. But, you should ask him for yourself, Cathy. Open up to him."

"I am already very open with him, Amy," I replied.

"No, ask him whatever comes in your heart, be free with him, be open with him, do not hold back. Get all your hesitations out of the way. This is a very, very special time for you and you will not realise its value till it is gone. Take it as a piece of advice from me. Try and get the maximum benefit of the time that he is spending with you now. Ask him whatever you feel from inside, anything you need to clarify, anything you want more details of."

"Tell me more about his life, Amy."

"His life? You want to know more about his life? I remember when I used to ask him the same question. Tell me more about your life, Suraj, I would say to him. And he would always put me off. For many months, he kept the details of his own life hidden from me but eventually just before he left, he told me all that I wanted to know. I remember all those times very clearly."

"Then tell me about it now." I pursuaded her.

"What do you want to know?"

"Tell me where he grew up. How he came to be on this path. How did he become what he is? Start at the beginning, Amy. I want to know all about his life."

"I don't know, if I can tell you all about his life, Cathy, because I don't think I know all about it. But I shall try to tell you as much as I do know.

"From what I have heard, he was born and brought up in India. He was born into a rich family. His father had built a business empire starting from scratch. Suraj is the younger of two brothers. And while he was growing up, till about the age of eighteen, there was very little spirituality or anything even close to that in his life. He grew up having the best the world had to offer as a result of his father's wealth. I know that he finished his studies in India and then came to the US to go to college. He readily admits that he had a fantastic time here and tremendous worldly fun, materialistic pleasure, and personal growth through relationships during his years in college.

"But towards the end of his stay in the US, he started to realise that having the best that the world had to offer was still not giving him any lasting inner peace or happiness. He realised that a fancy apartment, a great car, relationships with beautiful women, parties every night and a lot of money could not give him what he really sought—a lasting peace in his heart and a happiness he could carry with him everywhere all the time.

"It was at this time, I believe, that he read a book which described the experiences of a spiritual master from India. And that book changed Suraj. The truths which were mentioned in the book, the distinctions which were given between the external and the internal world, the ways that were described to reach everlasting happiness touched his heart. It was as if something long lost was being recognised. From that day, he started becoming less and less interested in the parties and the women.

"Material pleasures started losing their charm. Eventually, over a period of time, he would have parties, he would be among friends drinking, dancing, enjoying himself, and he could identify with none of it. He knew it was not the true him. When the time came for him to return to India, he went back with a sincere desire to associate with people who had a larger understanding of the spiritual side of life.

"Once back in India, he searched and sought out such people. He read all that he could about spiritual matters and the different paths towards the realisation of the self. In the meantime, he also got involved with his father's business, as was his father's desire. And he turned out to be a keen and energetic salesman and a successful businessman. Their business involved export and as a result, he was in touch with many foreigners from different parts of the world. He blended with them very well because of the kind of education he had received. He travelled widely on business and at the same time, wherever he went he sought out higher truths and people who had experiences of the spirit and could help him further along the way.

"Once, while he was in India, he came across the author of the first spiritual book he had read while in college. And at that moment, he recognised that man as his spiritual master. As he told me, Cathy, it was an inner feeling—a feeling which came to him not from his mind, but instinctively and openly from his heart. He just knew! He did not have to question, he did not have to think, he did not have to evaluate, he just knew that it was so. And his master confirmed the feeling.

"Since then, he has been on this path. Every once in a while, like you and I come to seek clarifications, he too returns to his master. Even though I personally don't feel that he needs any more clarifications in life, he seems to feel that he does.

"One of the things that he often tells me is that we are all teachers and students in this life, at one time or another with one person or another and it should always remain so. I cannot remember how many times he has told me this. From what I can see of him, he never wants to stop growing, never wants to stop being a student himself. He seeks out different masters of different faiths to talk with, to expand his knowledge, his understanding, and many times, I believe, even to clarify certain doubts which they may have."

"What about his family? Tell me more about his family," I asked Amy.

"As far as I know, Cathy, he is married and has two children, both sons. I have seen a photograph of him with his wife and kids, and his wife is truly beautiful. She is also of Indian origin, but was born and brought up away from India. And Suraj tells me that since he himself was part Indian and part foreigner, in that he was educated and grew up abroad for many years of his life, he feels that his wife was the perfect companion and mate for him."

"But, what kind of relationship do they have? Are they always happy? Didn't they have problems like we all do in our relationships?"

"Of course they did. From what he told me, the first couple of years after marriage went by as if in a dream. He was totally for her and into her, and she reciprocated in the same way. But after that all the problems started.

The reality that they were two different people started setting in. Over a period of time, they became so far apart that they were operating from completely different levels. Their motivations became different, their way of expression became different and there was lack of communication between the two.

"Suraj often tells me that in a man-woman relationship, communication is the key to understanding each other and growing together. 'If you can talk to each other openly and freely without fear or without judgement, then you can grow together,' he says. And that was what was lacking in their relationship. His wife is a wonderful person. He is the first to admit it. But, what happened was that they were growing in two completely different directions. As a result, there were fights, misunderstandings and arguments every day. There was no comfort or peace in the house. Love was there between the two, but it was never expressed. And slowly they drew apart. In the meantime, they had two children, both of whom were blessed by the masters even before birth.

"Has he talked to you about sex yet, Cathy?" Amy asked me.

"Sex? No, not yet. But what does sex have to do with spirituality?"

"A lot. But ask him. Let it come from him rather than from me." Amy said.

"Tell me more. So what happened in his marriage then? Is it still the same or did it improve?"

"No, it's not the same anymore. They had their own share of problems and there was even a time when they separated. But, you should see them now when they are together. They are so full of love for each other, so understanding of each other, and so giving to each other. When I see them together, which is only once in many years, I wish all relationships could be like that," Amy said.

"But how did it happen? How did it turn around?" I asked.

"For many years it didn't. They went through four or five very bad years. Within the bad years, there were some good moments, but there were lots of bad moments. They tried to talk to each other. Suraj tried to explain to her the meaning of a relationship—the reason, the purpose why two people get together in the first place. But, like I told you before, it was as if they were both operating from two entirely different levels. They both had a need to be loved, to be supported, to feel secure in each other's love, to feel wanted and appreciated. They both wanted to express their love and to see and feel the partner's love. But, they could never do it in harmony. One would attempt to do it, the other would misunderstand. One would try to say something, to get a feeling across, the other would take it the wrong way. So, they went through a number of bad years.

"But eventually, during one of the times when they were away from each other, they realised that they could not live without each other's love. They realised their priorities and the reason why two people get into a relationship like marriage where they commit themselves to each other for the rest of their lives. How did it happen, you asked me? Suraj says that the only reason it happened is because of God's grace. He says he had tried his best for so long that both of them should be happy, in peace, giving full love and receiving full love from each other and it had not worked, that eventually, when it did, he could attribute it only to the grace of God that the understanding had been created in their minds, the knowledge and the awareness had been given to them. That is what he says," Amy answered.

"I would like to meet his wife and children some day," I said.

"You may, some day you just may," came the reply from Amy. "But, tell me now about your relationship. Suraj told me about your husband. But, tell me, woman to woman, how is your marriage?" she asked.

"Frankly, not too good," I replied. "I think, I have the same problems as Suraj did. I try very hard to get my feelings across to my husband. But it never seems to work. I try to tell him what my needs are. But he never seems to understand. I also try hard to understand him, his needs, his behaviour and his moods. But, in spite of all my efforts, we just can't see eye to eye and that causes a lot of friction and disharmony between us, Amy. I know that the love is there. I know, Nick loves me and I love him too. From the bottom of my heart I love him too. But somehow we just can't make each other understand this. Do you have any suggestions?" I asked.

"No, there is no need for me to give suggestions," Amy replied. "Now that Suraj is in your life, start believing that everything will get better including your relationship with Nick. Let me just tell you one thing. He is here not only to change you, but also to bring about a change in Nick. He did the same when he came into my life. He interacted with me directly. But my husband changed too. Even though Suraj met him only a few times, the amount of change he brought about in my husband was tremendous. My relationship with him today is far, far better, though I can't say that it is perfect. But it is far, far better than it was before I met Suraj.

"So stop worrying, Cathy, and start believing that from this day on everything in your life is going to get better. You are getting stuck in negatives, thinking that your life is going to get worse or it is never going to get better, it is only going to get worse. You know that by now, I am sure."

"Yeah, Suraj did tell me something like that," I said.

"And what he told you is true. So, stop thinking negatively and start thinking that everything in your life is going to get better from this moment on. Just believe it! Believe it without an iota of doubt. Believe it a 110 per cent, and you will see that it happens.

"Enough, enough for now, Cathy. Let us go out and grab a cup of coffee before Suraj returns," Amy said, standing up.

"But there is so much more I want to know about him," I pleaded.

"Don't worry, there will be plenty of time later on. All that you want to know, you will know. Let's go now before he returns," Amy said, moving towards the door.

Suraj was back already when we returned to his room. He stood up as we entered and asked us how we had spent our time.

"Oh! we were just chit-chatting," I replied.

He looked into Amy's eyes for a minute or two, smiled, and without saying a word to her, turned to me and said, "She told you about my life, didn't she?"

No matter how much time I spent with him, I continued to be amazed by his ways.

"Yes, she did," I replied. "But just a little bit. There is so much more I want to know."

"What you need to know, Cathy, will come in time," he said. "But you must understand that what is important here is your life and how it is to be changed. Not my life and how it was changed. You need to spend more time working out your life rather than trying to find out what happened in mine."

"I understand that, Suraj. But, knowing what happened with you, I think, will inspire me and help me to change my life. Don't you agree?"

He didn't reply. Rather, he changed the subject completely and asked, "So, are we ready to go jet-skiing?"

Amy jumped up from the sofa, "Yes, I'm ready. Let's go."

"Let's leave then," Suraj said.

They didn't even give me a chance to speak. They were both moving towards the door, so I followed.

We spent the rest of the day jet-skiing and returned in the evening. The first chance I got to be alone with Amy, I said, "Did you see how he behaves when he is having fun? He is just like a small child. How can he be like that, Amy? How can he be a grown-up and a child at the same time? It amazes me, you know."

"Just accept that he is like that," Amy replied. "And if he continues to amaze you, be amazed. What is wrong with that? Maybe this amazement that you feel at his personality is part of your learning and your changing. So just accept it. Do not resist."

"Yes, but I have never seen anyone like him before."

"Neither had I when I first met him. But, believe me, there are a few others like him in this world. Just a few though. But, none of them is exactly the same as him."

"Tell me, Amy, what does he do in life for a living? I mean, he can't go around travelling the world, meeting different people, teaching them, changing lives, as he told me he does, without any kind of fixed income. What does he live on, if this is all he does?" I asked.

"You make it sound as if he does so little, Cathy. Is changing lives something small to do?" Amy said and added, "I have realised that it is easier to make a fortune or to build an empire rather than to change one life around and Suraj goes around changing so many of them. I don't think he is performing a small task. In fact, I feel it is a very noble, worthy and selfless act that he performs. And as far as his livelihood goes, I once asked him about it. And you know what he replied? As usual, speaking in spiritual terms, he said, 'When you follow the Father's orders, it is the Father's duty to make sure he sustains you while you follow his orders.' That was the reply I got. I didn't ask him anymore. If you wish to find out more, I think it is better you ask him directly," Amy said.

We left it at that.

In the evening, we dropped Amy at the airport for her return to Minnesota and were driving back when Suraj said, "I meant to ask you earlier about your job. What did your boss say when you applied for the leave?"

"He didn't say anything, Suraj. He was busy with some paperwork when I approached him. So he just signed my leave application, grunted a few words and went back to his papers," I answered.

"So he allowed you the leave. Didn't he?"

"Yes, if you look at it that way, he did allow it."

"The Lord works in mysterious ways," he said. "All good for us, but mysterious ways."

"Can I ask you a question, Suraj?" I said.

"Of course, Cathy," he replied. "You can ask me anything you want without hesitation."

"Why do I see you mostly in jeans? What's the reason?"

"Because they are practical, long-lasting, easy to care for and tough. Why else?" he replied. "What other reason could be there, Cathy? Just as you have to be practical in the mental attitude that you keep with yourself in life, so too in the things you keep around you, you must be practical and think of simplicity and effectiveness. That is the reason why you see me often in jeans."

We drove for a couple of minutes in silence and then he said, "I want to meet Nick tomorrow. What time do you think would be suitable for me to see him?"

"I am not sure he is willing to meet you, Suraj. We've been speaking occasionally about you and I think he has his doubts about who you are and what you do. I don't think my explaining you to him helped any. So I wonder if he would be willing to meet you."

"Why are you worried about that, Cathy? That is not your problem, Whether Nick is willing to meet me or not, is not your concern. Just tell me what would be a suitable time, according to you, for me to meet him. I'll take care of the rest. Don't you remember when we first met — you didn't really want to meet me either? Remember how much coaxing I had to resort to just to get you to have a cup of coffee with me?" he said jokingly.

I smiled at the memory, and then replied, "He leaves for work around eight in the morning. If you want, you can drop in at that time and take it from there."

"Good," he said. "Eight o'clock it is. Don't tell him that I will be coming. Growth always happens faster if it comes as a surprise."

> *All the problems you*
> *face in your lifetime have a*
> *lifetime of their own!*

13

LOVE, RELATIONSHIPS AND MARRIAGE

At five minutes to eight the next morning, the doorbell rang.

When I opened the door, it was Suraj. Nick was sitting in the hall having a cup of coffee when Suraj walked in.

"Suraj is here," I told Nick.

It seemed to me that Nick was surprised, angry and a bit amazed, all at the same time. He stood up and walked towards us.

Suraj put out his hand and said, "Hi! I am Suraj. I wanted to catch you before you left for work. I hope I came at the right time."

Nick shook his hand, gestured for him to sit down and then asked him, "Why did you come here at this time and what do you want?"

"I just wanted to meet you," Suraj replied. "And, I thought that morning would be a good time to catch you before you left the house. It seems that you are leaving for work soon and if you don't mind, I will come along for the ride."

"You want to ride with me to work? What purpose will that serve? Where do you have to go?" Nick asked.

"Well, I'll just come with you for a drive till your place of work. That way we can spend some time together in the car, and then I will take a cab back or something. Don't worry about me. I just want to spend some time with you. I am sure, Cathy has been talking to you about me by now." Suraj was his usual enthusiastic self.

"Yes, she has, and from her words it seems that you are some sort of Indian guru who suddenly decided that we need your help," Nick retorted.

"Why don't we leave?" Suraj said standing up. "We can talk on the way."

They left the house and just before Suraj got into the car, he looked back, smiled and waved to me. The message I got was, "Don't worry, everything will be all right."

They got into the car and left. What I am writing now about the time Suraj spent with Nick is actually how Nick described it to me later.

Once they were in the car, Suraj told him, "So you believe I am some sort of Indian guru. That's how you put it. Do you know the meaning of the word 'guru', Nick?"

"No, I don't know the exact meaning. But, I do know that gurus normally preach religion and they tell you about all kinds of things which we are supposed to follow to lead a better life."

"If you are interested, I can tell you the correct meaning of the word," Suraj asked gently.

"Go ahead," Nick said and looked away.

"The word 'guru'," Suraj clarified, "comes from the ancient language of Sanskrit. Sanskrit was the language which was used in India many, many years ago, and in fact most of the spiritual texts have been written in the Sanskrit language. The word 'guru' is made up of two different words together, 'gu' and 'ru'. Put together, it means 'the dispeller of darkness'—one who brings light in the darkness of ignorance. This is what the word 'guru' implies. Anyone who comes into your life and who is able to clarify or bring light to your confusion, to explain things to you, is termed a guru. Now, if you take it in the traditional sense of the word, I am a guru. But if you take it in the sense that people today have begun to see the word guru—like you said earlier, people who preach religion and create cult followings—then I am not a guru in that sense.

"Now that I have explained this meaning to you, Nick, let me ask you another question. Why do you have this hostility towards me? I

am talking to you man to man now and
sincerely, like your friend. Tell me, why do
you have this hostility towards me?" Suraj
asked.

"My friend? How can you be my friend?
You have just come into my life. You have
known my wife for some time, but not me. So
how can you be my friend?" Nick literally
shouted.

"Is that the reason why you feel hostile
towards me? Because Cathy has been
spending time with me? Is it because you
think I am here to take Cathy away from you?
Is this the reason why you are hostile, Nick?"

"No, that's not it at all," Nick retorted.

Suraj went on as if he hadn't heard, "But
let me tell you that I am not here to take
Cathy away from you, but rather to literally
give her to you. I mean this in the sense that
she must become fully aware of why she is in
this relationship with you, Nick, and then
voluntarily she will be here fully, one
hundred per cent. The full Cathy will be
available to you. But to have that, you must
understand also the importance of this
relationship that you are in. You must also be
present to her a hundred per cent. Without
that it will not happen. Do you understand
what I am trying to say?"

Nick didn't reply.

Suraj continued, "Do you know why two
people have a relationship? Do you know why

a man and a woman decide to have a relationship whether they be married or not?"
"Because they love each other. Isn't that the reason?" Nick said.
"That is what they think the reason is. But, tell me what is love, and even if you feel love, why commit? Why have this commitment in a marriage or in a relationship that you will be faithful to each other and not involve any third person in it? Can't you love and be with ten people at the same time? I want to understand what you think, Nick. What do you think the motivation is behind this relationship of a man and a woman?" Suraj asked.
"Well, marriage is something that you get into when you want to settle down, isn't it?" Nick said, "When you decide you want to have a family or you want to settle down with just one woman, you have to get married. It is a social institution and it has been this way for many, many years in our world. So, why tell me it is something which is not correct?" Nick asked.
"I am not saying it is not correct. Please don't misunderstand me. In fact, what I am saying is that it is an extremely valuable tool towards the growth of your soul. Now, here is my opinion and see if you agree with it or not. Two people get into a relationship voluntarily. They decide that here is the person they would like to spend the rest of their life with

and to be faithful to. Two people agree to live together, eat together, sleep together, wake up together and do so many other things throughout their life together with each other. For what?

"Every relationship has its own problems. There is no relationship which is perfect in this world, and the reason for that, Nick, is that two people cannot be alike. Two individuals, each with his own good and bad, each with his own defects and assets, come together and decide to live together. For what? You have two sets of goods and two sets of bads and these two sets don't match each other. The two goods that the two individuals bring into the relationship also do not match. In fact, you actually have four sets here working in a two-person relationship. Two sets of good and two sets of bad, and none of these four sets match any other. There are bound to be problems and there is bound to be friction in any relationship on this planet."

"I know that," Nick said.

"Do you also know that it is in the working out of this friction, in the smoothening of the problems that the key lies? Two people get into a relationship and the first hint of a problem that arises either distances them or breaks up the relationship completely because neither of the two is willing to give in, or rather, give up any of his or her own ideas and opinions. If they give in, it is in a sense of tolerance or because they have no other choice. They give in because they have no other way to go.

"But a relationship to be true to its purpose has to be about giving, about giving voluntarily, openly and lovingly, and not about giving in as a choice which you make because you have no other choice. That makes the relationship restricted and forced. When you give as in terms of wanting to give, it makes the relationship open, free and expansive.

"Relationships are actually the playground of God. You see, Nick, in this world, the fastest way to grow is by being involved in a relationship. Living together with a person, interacting with a person, being dedicated to the person, even if he hurts you and giving of your own love freely and openly, regardless of what the other person may do, is the secret of good relationships. Relationships are meant to balance and to develop us. They bring about the growth of both individuals involved in the relationship.

"Also remember that as you go through a relationship, at every moment you have a choice. The choice is between love and non-love. Everything you do can be done with an attitude of love or it can be done in an attitude of non-love. And this choice is something which one has to make at every step consciously. You have to decide and you have to follow your decision in seeking love in whatever you do," Suraj said.

"But, doesn't that make the relationship rather one way, Suraj? What happens when one person doesn't love and one person has the understanding that you are talking about? Then what happens?" Nick asked.

"You see, two people can never be on the same level of understanding. That is a given factor. But you must also know and believe in your heart that relationships are never a random occurrence. You must have read the *Bible* where it is written that there is nothing under the heavens which happens without a proper purpose or without a proper time. You can also presume and accept the fact that even relationships have a purpose and a time, and they are not happening as a random occurrence. So, once you get into a relationship with a person, it does not really matter what your partner is doing or what your partner's level of understanding is. If you are on a spiritual path, you must learn to see your mate as a spiritual being, one who is living with you for your own growth though she or he may be at a different level of growth himself," Suraj explained.

"But isn't it difficult then to live in harmony if two people are at completely different levels and they have problems at every stage? How is it possible to continue like that?" Nick asked Suraj.

"The solution to that is only one. From your own being, from your own perspective, you have to first see only your own spiritual growth within the relationship. You must first accept the other person's faults and bad points. Remember that we all have them. You must have faith that he or she is also originating in God and that you have to get along and accept him or her as he or she is. There is no other way.

"Now, this will be a struggle. Accepting a person is a tremendous struggle because you always go into a relationship with expectations. You want the person to be like this or that. You have a certain fixed idea in your mind and this idea has no flexibility. If your partner fits into this particular mould that you make, you are happy, and if he or she doesn't, then you are not happy. So, it is always a struggle to first accept a partner as he or she is. But, after you have accepted, after you have passed through this phase of struggling to accept, you will start seeing that the other person has some good points also. And, again remember that we all have good points. Once you reach this stage, getting along will no longer be a task for you or a struggle. It will no longer be a sacrifice. It will rather become an enjoyment and a voluntary act of giving all the time. That will bring you to a stage where, while you are in this relationship, you see God in your wife and your children and in everybody around you. Would you like to hear a small story?" Suraj asked.

"You bet," Nick replied.

"You know, in ancient India, there was once a powerful man who decided that he wanted to give up all worldly desires and start on the path of the soul's growth. He left his family, his business, his children and decided to renounce the world. After doing so, he went to the Himalayas. The Himalayas are the highest mountains in the world and also a spiritual powerhouse because they have been energised over thousands of years by different people meditating there.

"Well, this man went to the Himalayas and there he did severe penance, regular meditation and developed a very strong will. All kinds of powers came to him after years and years of doing this penance. And, once he felt that he had all the powers he wanted to achieve and had mastered himself, he got up from the mountains and decided to walk down and enter the city.

"On his way down, while he was walking under a tree, a bird sitting on the branches chose that particular moment to relieve itself, and the droppings fell on this man's shoulder. Just that simple act of nature made him so angry because of his pride in himself, in his own discipline and his achievement of power that he could not accept the fact that a simple little bird could actually defile his body.

"He looked up at the tree and saw that the bird was sitting there singing away. So through his power of will and the energy that he had developed, his gaze burnt the bird down.

"The man didn't even think twice about what he had done and continued to walk on. When he came to the first house below the hills, he knocked at the door. A lady opened it. When she saw that it was a holy man, she bowed before him and said, 'What can I do to help you? Please tell me.'

" 'I am hungry, please get me some food,' he ordered in a strong voice.

"Now, this lady could immediately make out what kind of person this man was. She told him, 'You will have to wait for half an hour because I am feeding my husband and after that I have to feed the children and only after that will I be able to give food to you.

"This was too much for the holy man to bear. He flared up and in all his ego, he told her, 'Do you know who I am? I have so much power.'

"And before he could say anymore, the lady of the house told/ him, 'I know just who you are but don't think I am like that little bird you burnt down with your gaze.'

"The man was completely shocked. How did this woman know what had happened just twenty minutes ago? How could she see? After all, she was a simple housewife. He fell at her feet and begged her forgiveness. He said to her, 'I realise that my ego and my pride have carried me away. I have wasted years and years sitting up in the mountains by myself. I have developed control over powers but no control over myself. Please tell me how you have developed yourself.'

"The woman said, 'To develop spiritually, one does not need to go away to the mountains, renouncing everything and leaving everything behind. To gain mastery over yourself, the ideal ground is the family, because in a family you have to deal with so many different relationships at one time. And in each of those relationships you have to give up of yourself. Giving up is the most difficult thing to do. But that is how I have been able to develop my own soul.'

"What do you think of this story, Nick?" Suraj asked.

"It's kind of nice and I tend to agree with what you are saying. But tell me, Suraj, what happens when the relationship is already going downhill? What happens when both the partners start feeling that the relationship is really approaching a stage which is beyond repair?" Nick said.

"Nick, please, my friend, listen to me. Troubled relationships actually mean that the ground and environment have been created by God for the growth of both the individuals involved. But, to really grow from this environment, they must see it this way and they must work to ease and to harmonise the relationship. Which again means that each of them must give up some of his or her own fixed notions and ideas. They must given up a part of themselves in faith and love to the other person," Suraj answered. "They must start thinking more about the other than of themselves."

"But, who starts first? After all, one of them has to take the first step forward." Nick asked.

"Again I tell you, Nick, two people come with different levels of intelligence and different levels of growth. You must always remember that 'improvement' begins with the letter 'I'. Always remember this. So, if you have the intelligence, you also have the responsibility to improve yourself first before your relationship can improve.

"Always keep in mind that we are not just physical beings having a spiritual experience. We are, in fact, spiritual beings having a physical experience. A relationship is a physical experience which two spiritual beings are having. Keep this in mind and it will become easier for you to create changes within the relationship — to make things more harmonious and smooth."

"But why do relationships hurt so much?" Nick asked.

"Remember that when a relationship is troubled and you are hurt, it is only because there is something inside you which is touched by whatever your partner does, something inside you or rather a loose end has been pulled by your partner and that hurts you. There is something you are not willing to accept about what your partner has said or done.

"I remember my master once demonstrating this to me. You know what he did? I was sitting at his feet and he had a napkin in his hand. He picked up the napkin and told me, 'Watch what I do, Suraj,' and then he threw the napkin on the wall with all his strength. Now, what happens when a cloth napkin hits the wall? Obviously, it just falls down. Then my master looked at me and said, 'What happened?' I didn't know what to reply to him, Nick. So, I said, 'It just fell down.'

"He asked, 'Why?'

"I told him, 'Because there was nothing there for the napkin to stick on.'

"He said, 'Well, it's the same with us in our lives and our relationships. If somebody throws something at us, and there is nothing inside us which will make it stick, nor anything inside us on which it can hang, then the thing just falls down. It is only when there is a nail up on the wall on which the napkin can hang, that it stays there.'

"It is the same with relationships, Nick! Whenever a partner does anything in a relationship, it is only if there is something inside us which is touchy, which is not willing to accept or which holds on to what they say that the hurt, the pain, the misunderstanding and the disharmony is caused. Otherwise, the thing just falls down and that never makes an effect, never makes a difference to us. In a relationship, the walls that you put up to hide incomplete parts of you are the same walls that stop love from reaching you and making you complete."

"So according to you, Suraj, what is the correct way to be in a relationship?" Nick asked.

"First of all, Nick, I am talking out of experience. I too have a wife and children. And things didn't always go smoothly for me either. We had a number of troubled years. I had to work at my relationship, just as hard as anybody else I know. But it is those of us who are willing to change that make the progress. If you are willing to grow and learn, progress is possible, otherwise it is not. So, believe that whatever I say to you today is out of experience.'

"What is the correct way, you asked me. The correct way is of giving love, not keeping it inside you. Remember that love is not love till you give it away. It is keeping in mind that your partner is being given to you for a certain purpose. That you both are in this relationship for a certain purpose. Both of you must be honest and open and giving to each other. You must have good communication. I see that in your country particularly, the pace of life has increased so much and people are so obsessed with externals that they allow relationships to be left behind. But, Nick, my friend, relationships can never be second priority in your life.

"It is through relationships that one achieves happiness and contentment. It is only after you have achieved these, that you can go after the externals—a good car, a good house and a good job and everything else that you want. Because all these externals by themselves will give you no peace and contentment, if you are not happy and harmonious at home.

"So, don't give your relationships second priority, and in this fast pace of life, do not allow them to be left behind. Don't forget that when things are falling apart in a relationship, that is actually the time when the greatest growth can happen. If you make the choice of having the courage to remain open instead of just closing off, if you have the courage to keep loving instead of taking away your love, the greatest growth can happen between two people at the worst of times. That is the secret of relationships according to me.

"And this also reminds me of a small joke. Care to hear it?" Suraj asked.

"Yeah, go ahead," Nick replied.

"One evening at this bar, there was a young man, who was downing one drink after another. He was talking to the bartender about how bad his marriage was and how he and his wife could not see eye to eye. Sitting right next to him was a sixty-year-old man, who also had a drink in his hand. He was sitting there quietly, peacefully by himself, sipping his drink.

"So, eventually, he looks up and tells this young man, 'You know, I have been married for forty years now, and I must tell you that my marriage is very happy and peaceful.'

"The young man says, 'I have been married just five years and my marriage is so bad that I cannot even explain it to you.'

"You can imagine his state of mind from his reply.

"'What is the secret of your marriage?' he asks the old man. 'How come you have been able to make it so peaceful and harmonious for yourself?'

"The old man replies, 'It is because I have learnt the three magic words that are to be used in a relationship all the time. You must say these words to your wife all the time if you want peace and happiness at home.'

"The young man say, 'Are the three words 'I love you?'

"The old man looks at him and he says, 'No my friend, they are: Yes, I agree.'

"Many times even against your instincts and desires, these are the three words which you have to use to keep peace. Yes, I agree! Whenever troubled times come, whenever your wife wants you to follow a certain point, if you feel that you are the stronger one or if you feel you are the one who has greater understanding, then use these three words, 'Yes, I agree.' 'Yes, my darling, I agree.'

"Magic words, don't you think, Nick?" Suraj said.

"Yeah, magic words for sure, Suraj. But they are extremely difficult to use in a difficult time. I am sure, you agree too," Nick replied.

"Yes, they are difficult to use, I agree. But the first time you use them is always the hardest, and every time after that becomes just a little easier," Suraj answered.

"Okay, I think my office is just around the corner now. Do you want me to drop you off here or do you want me to get you a cab?" Nick said.

"Just pull up here and I'll get down. Don't worry about me."

"When do I see you again, Suraj?" Nick asked.

"I would have thought you might not want to see me at all after this talk Nick."

"No, it's nothing like that, you know. I never really thought that you were a bad guy or anything. It is just that I didn't know why Cathy was spending so much time with you. But, I think, I understand now. So, tell me what you are doing this evening, because if you are free, let us get together and go for dinner," Nick said.

"Yeah, that's fine with me. Let's fix it for dinner then, because my time left here is short and I need to eventually finish my task and get back. So, dinner would be fine."

"What time do you want to meet? How about 7.30 p.m.? Is it okay if I pick you up at 7.30?"

"That's just perfect," Suraj said.

So, Nick dropped Suraj off at the corner and then went to work.

Meanwhile, at home, I had called up Amy in Minneapolis. She had given me her telephone number before she left. She was happy I had called and we spoke about my time in the last few days.

"Why is he called Suraj?" I asked Amy. "I asked him earlier but he said he would tell me later. Do you know the reason? If you do, Amy, please tell me."

"Cathy, when Suraj had spent a lot of time on this path, one day his master called for him while he was sitting out in the garden. Suraj came and sat down. His master then looked up at the sun, pointed at it and told Suraj, 'Look at the sun, it shines on you and me alike. It shines on the trees, on the birds, on the birds, on the animals, on the rivers, and on the earth. It shines on people who are alive, people who are dying and even on dead bodies. It does not judge who deserves the sunlight and who doesn't. It does not ask who is good and who is bad. It only gives without asking. What does it give? It gives life, it gives energy, it gives light, it gives heat. It gives so much of its life every day to all of us without judging us, without seeing who deserves it and who doesn't and it does all these things without asking for anything in return. Be like the sun. From today on, try and be as much like the sun as you can. Do you understand?' his master asked.

"Suraj looked up into his master's eyes and replied, 'I shall try, my master. If you give me the strength. I hope I will be successful.'

"The master looked down at him with tears in his eyes. He held his head in his hands, put his forehead to Suraj's forehead and said, 'Not only will I give you strength, but the sun

itself and the whole universe and the Father
of us all, the Divinity behind everything, shall
stand behind your attempts. Go forth
fearlessly, for behind you stands immense
power. From today, you shall be called Suraj.'

"From that day, Cathy, his name has been
Suraj, which in the Hindi language means the
sun. In fact, I don't know his name before
that because even when I first met him, he
was called Suraj."

"Interesting story, Amy," I replied.

"That's the way it is," she said. "I have met
some other students of his and they told me
the same thing. His master gave him this task
of giving knowledge: to give light where
darkness prevails, to dispel ignorance, to give
warmth and love, and to make people aware
and thus alive wherever possible he can, to
whoever seeks the knowledge. And that is
what he has been doing ever since."

> *Relationships are the earthly
> playground of God. There,
> He teaches us playfully!*

14

SEX FOR THE SPIRIT

Nick called me from work. "We're having dinner with Suraj, Cathy," he said.

Once again, I was amazed. What power did Suraj have, I wondered. All these days, Nick had been completely against him mentally. He didn't want to meet him, didn't want to see him, didn't want to know anything about him or even what he was talking to me about. And, the first day they met, after spending just a couple of hours later, it was as if my husband's whole attitude had changed and he now wanted to spend more time with Suraj. I wondered what power Suraj possessed to bc able to change people's feelings and emotions so easily.

"How come?" I asked Nick.

"Well, we didn't have enough time on the way to the office, and I decided to invite him for dinner so that we could continue to talk."

"And where do you want to go for dinner, Nick?"

"Where do you suggest?" he asked.

"There is a good Chinese restaurant not far from here. Why not take him there?" I replied.

"Okay, I'll pick you up first in the evening and then we'll go get him," he answered.

At dinner that evening, Suraj ordered a couple of vegetarian dishes for himself. Both Nick and I felt a little awkward ordering non-vegetarian dishes for ourselves when we saw him ordering otherwise.

"No, please don't feel awkward. Please go ahead and order whatever you want," Suraj told us.

"But we can eat vegetarian today too," I said.

"Cathy," he said looking into my eyes, "what's the point of doing something only for one day? Please go ahead and order whatever you both want. It is quite all right. Please believe me."

So we ordered our regular favourite dishes. While we waited for dinner, the conversation continued.

"Were you always vegetarian?" Nick asked.

"No, in fact, I wasn't. I have always been extremely fond of good food since I was a child," Suraj replied. "One of my greatest pleasures, as I travelled around the world, was to go to different countries and try their native cuisine. I was so adventurous that I wanted to try everything new that I hadn't had before. For example, I've tried everything from octopuses to snakes to snails to different kinds of birds. But that was a long time ago. I've been vegetarian for many years now."

"But what's the reason?" I asked Suraj. "Did your master tell you to stop? I know that most people who are into meditation are vegetarian. Is that the reason for you too?"

"With me it so happened that one day I found I did not want to eat the flesh of another living being anymore. Now, my wife and I would go out very often for intimate dinners. Just the two of us. No one else. We would love to spend time with each other and enjoy good food together. But, one day, while I was sitting there eating some chicken, a thought came to my mind, 'Do I really need to eat the flesh of a chicken to exist, to survive?' And the feeling was extremely strong. But due to my cautious nature, I decided not to act on it right away but to wait and see if the feeling really deepened and matured.

"I let a few months pass like that. The feeling just continued to grow inside me all the time. Every time I went out with friends or with my wife or even when I ate alone, I felt that I could easily, and probably more comfortably, survive without eating the flesh of a living being. Eventually, after about three months, the feeling became so strong that one day I just made up my mind and my heart and gave up eating non-vegetarian food completely. It was not because my master told me to or because anybody else instructed me to. It was just because I had an inner feeling that I was not doing the correct thing."

"Does that mean that being non-vegetarian is wrong?" Nick asked.

"Oh no, not at all," Suraj replied. "In fact, the majority of the population of this world is non-vegetarian."

"Then what is the reason or the advantage in being a vegetarian?" Nick asked Suraj.

"Well, if you really want me to explain it to you, there are two main reasons. One is the spiritual reason and the other is just a worldly reason. Which one do you want me to tell you first?"

"Whichever one you like," Nick said.

"Then I'll tell you the worldly reason first. Nick, man is not as strong as the many hundreds of animals around him. He is not as fast. He is not as deadly. But, one thing is for sure. The advantage he possesses over everybody else is his intelligence and his awareness. Now, having this intelligence, he uses the tools that he has created to overpower the animals around him and then he uses them to satisfy his own desires. In nature, if you put up one individual against the other, one man by himself probably cannot even kill a monkey. But with the weapons he has developed, one man today with an automatic rifle can go and massacre a hundred monkeys at one time for no real or valid reason, and the man with the rifle need not be strong or even smart. All that he needs to do is to point his weapon in the right direction and pull the trigger, and bodies start falling before him. Where is the fairness or the balance in this equation? It is just a case of unfair advantage being misused.

"Weapons give us power, but remember that if a man's mind is not under his control, this power is always misused. A man who goes hunting does not need to kill numerous animals to satisfy his hunger. And tell me one more thing, that if he has a choice of not killing anything, why would he need to kill a living animal with families, with children, to satisfy his own hunger? Men kill because of their egos, their pride or even because of their insecurities. They seek temporary thrills. Man was not designed to be a hunter or a killer.

"The reason why man has been given greater mind power over other animals is because he should not be as controlled by his instincts as animals are. When they feel hungry, they go and hunt. They kill only enough to satisfy their hunger. Man can plan ahead so that he never feels the need to go and hunt when he feels hungry. He uses his mind for this, or rather he should use his mind for this. But instead, a mind which is not controlled is used by man to imbalance the universal equation. Look at our teeth,

Nick. Are they designed to tear out meat like a predator's teeth are? Look at our hands. Do we have claws that can rip a face apart? Look at our bodies. How fast can we run? Man's body was designed for the sole purpose of the evolution of his mind and his awareness. That is the worldly reason. We need not really kill anybody for our own survival because of our greater intelligence and greater understanding. We can as easily use this intelligence and understanding to plan ahead so that we can survive without killing at all. We fail in our responsibility if we do not use our advantage for its intended purpose."

"And what's the spiritual reason?" I asked.

"You know very well that all bodies have hormones and also produce certain chemicals as a result of different reactions. What happens to us when we get angry? All of a sudden, we ourselves are very agitated. The emotion of anger inside you has signalled your brain to produce certain chemicals which then go into your bloodstream and make your body processes agitated. You become restless, you need to hit out at something, you need to get that extra energy out. It is a proven fact that the human body produces different chemicals for different reactions—reactions which are all motivated by our emotions. The same is true for animals.

"First of all, you must understand that animals are less evolved body forms than us. The package of the animal's mind, body and spirit together is at a level lower than yours and that is simply proved by the fact that they are not as aware as you are, and secondly, they are more controlled by instincts than by their intelligence. Therefore, a lower life form will obviously have lower emotions. For example, Nick, animals do not feel any emotions of patriotism or of love for the universe. There have been cases where animals have eaten their own newborn just for survival. Isn't that simply being led through your life without awareness and only by your own instincts of survival? And animals also carry with them the cumulative effect of all their actions and reactions just as we humans do. Only this balance in animals is of much cruder emotions than the balance of humans. When you eat an animal's flesh, what you are actually eating is a part of his body which is suffused with the chemicals that the animal's brain has produced. When an animal dies, be sure it is aware that it is dying. It is fearful, helpless and angry. So its body in the last throes of death produces the chemicals that are necessary for trying to survive or chemicals and enzymes which are related to the fear and helplessness the animal feels. These chemicals go into its body and remain there. Eventually, this is the same flesh that we eat and with it come two things. One, the chemicals that the animal has produced and which will affect us too and second, part of the karmic balance of actions and reactions that the animal went through in its life.

"When you are trying to heighten your own awareness, you don't want these lower and baser emotions coming into your body. That's the spiritual reason, Nick. Also, don't forget that spiritually it is wrong to kill anything just to satisfy ourselves.

"If we kill to protect, that's a different thing but killing another just to satisfy our hunger of killing anybody is wrong when you look at it from a spiritual angle."

I don't know how Nick was feeling. But the way Suraj explained things, all of a sudden, I didn't feel like eating the dishes I had ordered just a few moments ago. But Suraj kept right on talking.

"Have you spoken to Cathy about what I explained about relationships earlier today, Nick?" he asked.

"No, not yet." Nick replied.

So, Suraj updated me on the conversation that he and Nick had had in the morning. He told me the reasons why people get into human relationships, how the greatest growth for us on this earth can take place through interaction with people, rather than by being individually motivated or by individual existence. He showed me the purpose of problematic relationships and how to get out of them by keeping the correct attitude and by keeping our eyes on the goal rather than on the daily problems. After he had finished this, he popped a surprise question to both of us.

Sitting there across the table and smiling, he asked, "So, what do you both think about sex?"

I remembered Amy asking me if Suraj had spoken about sex yet, and a smile came to my face. I looked at Nick and saw him smiling too.

"Sex?" Nick said. "I think it's the greatest thing in this world."

Suraj accepted that and then looked at me. "And what do you think, Cathy? What's your feeling about sex?"

"Sex is great," I said. "But it's great only if two people love each other," I added.

"You know, I am really happy to see that you both enjoy the act of sex. But in all these years of being married and having made love to each other so many times, tell me truthfully, have you ever got the feeling that sex is very little about two bodies, and more about the emotions, the feelings and the souls that the two bodies house? As much as two physical bodies may want to love and satisfy each other always, the best they can do is to give momentary satisfaction. If the emotions are not touching, if the two souls are not touching each other, sex can never be satisfactory in the long-term," Suraj told us.

"I agree with you," I said.

"Then what is the way to make it satisfactory for a long, long time, Suraj?" Nick asked.

"Sex, you must understand, is an expression. An expression of what? It is an expression through your bodies of what is inside your bodies. Your soul thirsts for love and completion. Your emotions yearn to be expressed and fulfilled, and all of this is possible through sex. The act of sex is undertaken by two bodies, yes. But it should be two bodies and two souls along with all the emotions and feelings that they contain which must be expressed through sex. Only then does it even reach close to what its true purpose is."

"What according to you is the purpose of sex apart from enjoyment, bonding and procreating?" I asked Suraj.

"Cathy, tell me, what is the greatest energy that is available to man? Knowing that man cannot really create or really destroy, as I explained to you earlier, the greatest energy, because it is the only creative energy available to man, is the power of sex. I prefer to call it 'making love' rather than sex. It is only through the act of making love between two people of two different sexes, i.e., male and female, that creation can take place. Now you must also understand that a man and a woman, when in physical union, only create the physical body. The body, as I told you, is a vehicle for a soul. But only when they create a physical body does a particular soul have a chance of coming into this classroom of life and of using that body as a sensory expressive organ to live in and to function within this environment during its lifetime. It becomes a vehicle for him or her to give and to take, to sense and to express, to learn and to grow. Without a human body, it is impossible for a soul to exist in this plane and to have all the numerous lessons and sensory inputs that this world has to offer. And, it is only through the act of making love, through expressing the love that two souls feel for each other in a physical way, that the human body is created, and which then comes to house a soul. So, in effect, human beings can only create when they are having sex with each other," Suraj explained.

"But when it gives so much sensory satisfaction, how can it be only for the act of procreation? Tell me, Suraj," Nick asked.

"There are many other purposes of sex rather than just procreation," he replied, and then continued. "The act of making love is the chance of exploring the full potential of one's sexual energy through intimate and open physical sharing and expression. When two people get together to unite physically, to make love, it is an expression of literally giving yourself to the other person, of belonging to each other. A private bond is created between the two and it is expressed through their physical love.

"Making love is all about giving. It is not about taking. Both the partners involved receive pleasure. It is in opening yourself up, it is in expressing your feelings, it is in going to the areas which you have never opened to anybody else, and opening them in love and trust to the partner in front of you that the pleasure comes. That is what gives freedom because the walls are broken down. And whatever you open, remember, will give you freedom. The more you let go, the more freedom you get. The more you express, the more you will sense and the more you will receive pleasure in return. The basic premise, the basic motivation in the act of making love between two people is the act of sharing your inside, sharing your soul, expressing what is inside you and not putting up any walls or hiding any parts of your personality.

"Remember that once the outer barriers like clothes are shed, inner barriers are supposed to break down also. Communication links in all ways between two humans are supposed to improve. That is what the essence of making love is. That is what takes love into a higher plane. It is not just sex anymore. It now ceases to be only a mechanical act between two bodies which involves kissing, touching, holding, pressing, penetration, etc. It becomes an emotional act first and then it becomes a spiritual act."

"So are there three levels of physical love between man and woman?" I asked.

"Yes, the moment your inhibitions are left behind, all your walls come crumbling down. All fears must go and you must fully bare yourself, not only your body but your emotions and spirit too. Nothing must be hidden. The moment all barriers are removed, the relationship has a chance to be complete. Before that, it can never be complete. Sex has tremendous energy in it. But as long as that energy is used for a physical act only which eventually ends and releases the energy, it can never take your awareness higher. In fact, it brings your awareness and consciousness lower. But, once that act becomes an emotional act, a spiritual act, in which you are giving yourself, you are opening yourself up, in which you are expressing yourself, it becomes selfless. You want to give so much to your partner, and you also understand and realise at that moment that it is in the giving of yourself that you receive, that you yourself start to feel the pleasure every time you give.

"And when you are receiving in your giving, all inhibitions are overcome. Nothing, no secrets, physical or emotional, come between the two partners. Every part of the body, of the soul is seen, felt, smelt, touched, tasted and held by the partners until the two individuals unite into one. That is the secret of sex.

"Making love then does not remain a taking, selfish, physical act. It becomes a giving, expressing, selfless act, which is literally a form of prayer in itself. Through the body, the hearts are touched. Through the body, the emotions are opened. Through the body, the needs and the desires are expressed. Through the body, the fears are released. Through the body, the security is given, and through the body, the soul is merged. Through the act of physical sharing, God is revered and remembered," Suraj said. "Making love goes from the physical to the emotional and finally to a spiritual plane where it literally becomes a prayer to the Divine."

He seemed in ecstasy himself. We both listened to Suraj telling us his idea of what making love between two people is all about. We had dinner and then drove back home while conversation continued on one topic or another.

"Cathy, tell me, have you ever felt the desire to have children in all these years of marriage?" he asked as we neared his motel.

"You asked me that before, Suraj!" I replied. "And the answer is, yes, I have. I have had the desire, but we decided against it."

"And why not?" he asked.

"Well, we discussed it between the two of us," I answered, looking at Nick, "And felt that it was too early in the relationship. We felt that we needed to have a secure base professionally and to settle down a little bit more. And also to be more secure financially before we could have children."

"That's not a good enough reason," he told me, and then added, "You have been born a woman. A child can only come into this planet through you. When the desire comes out of itself into your mind, or into your body and is expressed as an emotion, you must understand that something more than yourself is talking to you. A soul takes birth as a woman to learn the lessons that a woman learns through this earthly classroom during her lifetime, to give things only a woman can give. And one of these things is the birth of a child. If you have felt the desire to give birth to children earlier, it means that it was time for you to have children. So, don't worry about all the other things of life, all the external material things. Learn to listen to your inner voice first. Everything else shall be added on to you."

"What are you saying? Are you telling me that it is the right time for me to have kids now?"

"What I am saying is that there is a soul out there whose destiny it is to be born through you as your child and it is waiting for you to make the decision to unite with your husband in physical union to create an avenue for it to be able to enter this earth. That is the only gateway, that is the only door that is open to a soul to enter a body. And this privilege is only given to a woman.

"A woman goes through different stages of life and a moment comes in her life when she feels an inner need and calling to be a mother. There is no woman on this earth who has not felt this need or calling at least some time in her life. Women may ignore it, women may deny it. But, it is always there in her life at some time or another. And, in fact, it is a very essential part of being a woman. So, why do you wait longer? Having a child now or whenever you both decide, since it should be a voluntary and willing decision from both of you, may in fact just change your external circumstances for the better. One never knows. You must choose to listen to your inner voice more than the outer world. The outer world speaks to you of things which are worldly and materialistic. The inner world speaks to you with the voice of your spirit, of your soul, of your emotions. Which would you rather listen to?"

After this, the conversation changed to other mundane things. We talked with Suraj throughout the drive. Later, we dropped him at his motel, when he told Nick to pick him up again the next morning on his way to work.

"I have a few more things to discuss with you, Nick, before I leave," Suraj said.

On the way back home, I asked Nick, "What did you think of all that Suraj spoke about?"

"I am amazed at how much he seems to know, and he is so young. And sometimes I really doubt if he is speaking from experience. I wonder if he is just making everything up. How can one so young speak so deeply of so many things? After all, Cathy, we have grown up too. We have lived in a fast-paced society, in a modern culture. We've been through everything that life has to offer. So, I really wonder where all his knowledge comes from and if it's true. But then, what he says makes so much sense that one really can't deny it either," he said.

I had to agree with that. I had been through the same feelings about Suraj when I met him initially. The first few days I had thought that same thought numerous times. But, in spite of all the doubts that my mind put up, what really made me keep listening to him, keep having faith in his words, was the fact that he didn't ask for anything in return. All his talk, all his actions, all of his time that he spent with us, was really just an act of giving to us. That is what, more than any other reason, always made me carry on listening, and having faith in what he said.

> *Making love, is more*
> *about two souls and their*
> *emotions than about two bodies!*

15

THE STRENGTH OF A WOMAN

The next morning, Nick picked up Suraj on his way to work. "Thanks for picking me up," Suraj said, "because there is one other thing I must talk to you about."

"What's that?" Nick asked.

"Nick, have you really ever wondered why there are women on this earth? Why not only men?"

"Well, obviously if there were only men," Nick replied, "where would we come from? Like you were telling us last night, the only way a soul can come into this world is through a woman."

"That's a good answer, and it's true. But, there is another reason. Want to know what it is?" Suraj asked.

"Sure, go ahead," Nick replied.

"Have you ever heard of the concept of Yin and Yang?"

"No, not really," Nick said. "What's that?"

"Yin and Yang is basically a Chinese Taoist concept. But, if you look at it deeply, it's true for every culture and every religion. What it essentially means is that in every being, in every soul, there are both the feminine and the masculine parts. But, in each individual, one of these is more prevalent than the other. For example, let us take us Nick. We are men, male. But, within us is also a certain small portion of feminine qualities. All those qualities which are soft, gentle, yielding, embracing, tolerating, compassionate, loving, are feminine qualities, and all the parts which are more powerful, which are cruder, which are hard and harsh, like aggressiveness, determination, competitiveness, penetration, all of these are masculine parts. A woman works best with emotions and a man with logic. Every soul comes into this earth with a certain ratio between these two qualities and the experiences we need to grow and become more complete determine whether we are going to be male or female in this birth.

"So, that makes you realise that you as a male have a majority of masculine qualities, but a certain minority of feminine qualities, and Cathy, as a female, has a majority of feminine qualities and a certain minority of masculine qualities. The reason men and women exist together on this earth is for the growth and fulfilment of each other. A man can only find fulfilment and completion on this worldly plane through a woman. When a man and a woman have united in harmony— and I am not talking only about physical union but when they are living together, truly in love with each other and expressing it every day of their lives in every way—that is the closest they come to understanding what God's love is like.

"Around this love between one man and one woman, a family is built. If the love between these two at the centre of the family is strong enough, that love can then radiate outwards and encompass greater and greater areas, and an increasingly larger number of people. That love between the two of them provides each one greater security, and greater freedom and completion. When a man is with a woman, both his feminine qualities and masculine qualities are enhanced. They become greater. He becomes more aware. Understand this. It is energies we are talking about here. When a man is with a woman, she looks up to his masculine qualities, and when she does, he feels like expressing them more and more but in a more tolerant and controlled manner. So, his masculine qualities become more focused. Also, when he sees in her the feminine qualities, he feels like expressing his feminine qualities also. So, both the masculine and feminine qualities of a male are expressed, enhanced and focused more when he is with a female.

"It is the same with a female. Her feminine qualities are expressed better and are more focused when she is with a man because in expressing those, she feels more pleasure and happiness, and she gives more satisfaction to the male. She also feels more secure when she expresses her feminine qualities. But, when she sees the masculine qualities in the male, she tries to experience her masculine qualities also. It is good for both the male and the female when this balance occurs."

"But don't you think, Suraj, that in this worldly, material society, one role or rather one sex has to be more powerful than the other?" Nick asked.

"Nick, powerful is a relative term. What do you call powerful? If a male picks a fight to prove himself at the drop of a hat or at the first insult thrown at him, do you call that powerful? Do you call that an act of strength? Or do you call the tolerance that a woman shows to all the pains and the pressures of a family, the love that she gives, the way she supports others around her in their troubles powerful? Powerful is a relative term. It depends on what society calls powerful that it labels one sex out of the two more powerful than the other. There have been societies and cultures in this world earlier which have actually called the female the more powerful of the two.

"Even today, in the East, there are cultures which really revere the female, even to the extent that they worship her in different forms as goddesses. The woman is given so much reverence because it is felt that she has a lot more to go through in her life. She has the capacity to bear more pain, to absorb a lot more into her system. At the same time, she has the ability to give more support to others than men do. You see, a woman who is strong inside, who has the ability to take more, also has the ability to give more. That absorbing makes her stronger and once she is stronger, she can give more to others. She can give more of her strength. I personally believe that women are the stronger of the two.

"Why do you think that, Suraj?"

"Nick, a woman is what a family is focused around. She has a lot more responsibility for the way the world is growing than a man does. Whether you can see this now or not, it doesn't matter, but just take it to be true. A culture remains stable if the women of the society remain stable. Things are preserved, values, emotions, and feelings are preserved in society, if they are preserved in the woman first. She has the ability to handle more pain, to absorb more sorrow, a lot more hurt, which eventually leads her to greater growth and makes her stronger. She also has the ability to support more, to love more and to strengthen the male and others around her. Also, don't forget that God saw only her good enough to be the doorway to this world. He probably knew that men couldn't handle the task.

"So, as we go through our relationships in life, Nick, it is good for us to remember the strength of women and their role when we interact with them. We must respect them, Nick, for what they are and in any case when two people respect each other, the relationship is always smoother. I personally feel that when souls have a choice of taking on either the male role or the female role on the physical plane, it is always the stronger souls who pick the female's role. The Earth is not called our Mother for nothing, you know. She is feminine because only then can she have the strength to continue to love, tolerate and support us even when we show little care for her. She is the epitome of woman. But then, again, that is my personal opinion and you need not believe it till you actually feel it," Suraj added. "And even though women are strong within themselves, do you know the real source of their strength?"

"No," Nick replied.

"I'll tell you a story, okay?" Suraj said.

"Sure."

"One day, a journalist read about a lady, 55 years old, who had brought up seven children, was running the house all by herself, and was the owner of a very large international organisation. The most amazing thing however was that she had been widowed a couple of years after her marriage.

"This journalist is amazed. He knows how difficult it is to live in this material world. He knows how difficult it is to make two ends meet and to fulfil the responsibilities of bringing up a family and living daily life. But this lady apparently has brought up many children and also runs an international business all by herself. So, the journalist decides that he must interview the lady and find out the secret. What is it that has made her strong enough to do so much in life?

"He fixes an appointment to see her and when the day comes, he goes there in anticipation of finding out this great secret.

"He is asking the lady different questions and she is sitting there answering him, very comfortable, relaxed, without any kind of tension at all. Finally the man asks her, 'Please tell me, what is it you attribute the success of your life to? What is it that has given you the strength to make so much out of your life? Because, being widowed at an early age, and bringing up so many children while running a business, is quite a task for a single parent.'

"The lady looks at him, smiles and says, 'You have asked me the question which is closest to my heart and the secret of it is that when my husband died, I had two children and I was completely broken down. Before that, I had led a completely protected life while I was with my parents and even after I got married. My husband always took care of the needs of the house, of the family and provided everything. I never really had a need or chance to become worldly-wise. When my husband died suddenly, I was completely broken and spent many days in despair without any hope and without seeing any kind of future for myself.

" 'But, then, I remembered that I had always been close to God and He had always helped me whenever I needed His assistance in my life. So, I sat down one night after many nights of crying and I spoke to Him. I told Him— God, I have kept You with me always: when I was growing up, when I was living with my parents, when I got married, I have always kept You with me, and You have always helped me. You gave me wonderful parents, You gave me a loving husband, You gave me such good children. So, I am again coming to You and asking for Your help. I am at a stage where I cannot go on alone by myself. I need Your help. Please remain with me and please support me—And after saying that, I also told Him—God, I will try to do the best in my life. But, You be my partner, You be my mate. I will do all the work. That's my job since I am here. But, please, You have to do all the worrying and the guiding. That is not my job. I cannot take responsibility for that.

" 'And, do you know, since that day, I started living my life again. I brought up my two children. I started a business, and in fact, there came a stage when I adopted children. I brought them up too. My business grew. I continued to work hard and I never really missed my husband for all the worldly needs and benefits. I miss him everyday for his love, his attention and his companionship. But I became self-sufficient. I would get up every morning, pray to God and tell Him— You worry and You guide me and let me do all the work—and that is how I have lived my life. He has been a partner in every single day of my life and in every task that I perform. He has been a most faithful partner in that He has always performed His task very well. I perform my duties, that is, the duty of working, and He performs his duties, that is, the duty of worrying about everything and of guiding me in my life. That is the secret of my success. With Him by my side, I am always in a majority.'

"Now Nick, I say to you — this is the easiest way to live your life. To flow through it, to go through good and bad, because both will come to you in your life. You must accept them. But, this is the easiest, simplest, fastest way to raise your consciousness, to make your life easier for you, to have good relationships and to become closer to your Father who always wants to be near you.

"Also, do not forget that every time you take one step towards God, He takes nine steps towards you. Look at the ratio here. It is not fair. Is it? But, then God is so full of love that He cannot ever behave towards His own children in a state of fairness. Does a child who comes to his father crying for a toy expect fairness from his father? The father's heart fills up with love and he forgets all about fairness and justice. He knows that he has to get his child whatever he needs. It is the same with God. When He sees you crying, the love in His heart for you just explodes. You take one step towards Him and He is so happy that you have taken that one step that He runs the nine steps towards you. Remember this secret."

> *With God by your side, you are always in majority!*

16

SIMPLIFY AND FLOW

The next day, both of us met Suraj over a cup of coffee. We reviewed the past few weeks that he had spent talking to us about things in a way we had least expected.

After the review, he said, "There are two more things I want to tell you, which I feel may help you in your growth at this stage. The first is, that the real success of anything lies in making your life simpler. People today have got used to having so much around them that in the end they end up with many things which are useless. Instead of simplifying their lives, they complicate them more and more. In the name of simplification, new things are bought and then things are bought to augment those things and then things are bought to maintain those accessories.

"Needs which never existed before are considered necessities today and in the end man becomes so encumbered and so laden down with things around him that he finds it difficult to live his own life. He ends up taking care of the things which should actually be taking care of him. So, try and simplify your life, both inner and outer, at every step.

"Happiness lies not in adding on things or material possessions to give you happiness. Rather, it lies in simplifying things and being happy with whatever you have. Happiness is never achieved by getting more but by giving up and letting go of more.

"There are two ways in which you can live life. First, add on things to fulfil your needs. But that never works because your needs also keep increasing. And the second way is to reduce your needs to fit in with the things that you have. That way always works. Obviously it is a little harder way and that is why most people avoid at. So, that's a first thing to remember—simplify, simplify, and then, simplify some more!

"The second thing to remember, as you go through life, its relationships and its many lessons and opportunities for growth, is that one must always keep flowing."

"You told us that before," I said.

"Yes, I know. But listen to it again because flow is very important.

"One day, a young girl came to my master. Her name was Kaveri. Kaveri is also the name of one of the rivers of India.

"She told my master, 'Please, Sir, tell me what is the way to live a happy life?'

"My master smiled at her and replied, 'My child, your name itself tells you the secret.

You are named after the great river Kaveri
and as the Kaveri always flows endlessly into
the sea, remember that as you go through
life, keep flowing all the time. Don't ever get
stuck. Sometimes the flow may be slow and
sometimes fast. But, keep flowing through
life. Don't take things too seriously. Don't get
stuck at any stage. If obstacles come, flow
over them or around them or under them.
But, keep flowing. Don't get stuck anywhere.'

"This is a valid and important lesson to
remember in our lives and relationships also.
Problems will come. No question about it. No
doubt about it. Each one of us has his or her
own problems, each relationship comes with
problems, each life has both good and bad.
Keep flowing through it all and you will find
that it all becomes easier for you. Remember,
the human body is alive as long as blood
flows. Once that flow stops, the body drops.
So too with life.'

"I have a story for you regarding the first
lesson of simplification, how the secret lies in
simplification rather than complication. Do
you wish to hear it?" he asked us.

"Of course," we replied together.

"Well, once in ancient India, there was a
master who had a very faithful disciple. The
disciple had undertaken severe penances for
many years under his master's guidance.
And, it was time for him to be alone, away
from his master. The master gives him

instructions for the next five years and asks him to go to a certain part of the forest to begin his practices in solitude. When the disciple is leaving, the master tells him, 'Keep your mind focused on my instructions. Keep the goal ahead of you all the time in view. Do not get attached to any other thing apart from the goal, which is your destination and what you must arrive at.'

"The disciple, with his last instructions, leaves for the forest to begin his practices. On his way there, he passes a river where he finds a puppy which has been badly injured. Apparently, the puppy had come to the river to drink water and was attacked by another animal. In the fight that ensued, it ended up with a broken leg. Now it was lying on the sand, not able to move and yelping away in pain. When the disciple saw this puppy, a feeling of pity and compassion rose within him. He thought to himself, 'My master has always taught me to give love and to be compassionate, to save life and to lend a helping hand to anybody in need. This is surely a test for me. How can I neglect this puppy now?' So the disciple picks up the puppy and takes it along with him into the forest.

"At his designated area, he builds a hut, bandages the puppy's foot with some medicinal herbs and starts his meditative practices. A few hours later, he is disturbed by the yelping of the puppy. The puppy is yelping because it is hungry. The disciple gets up from his meditation and goes to find some food for him. This carries on for a few days and eventually, the disciple is unable to meditate or perform his other practices. He decides that it is necessary for him to find someone else to take care of the puppy. Then he can be free to carry on with his meditation.

"He goes to find somebody to fill the need, and eventually hires an assistant to take care of the hut and also the puppy at the same time. He thinks to himself that the assistant can take care of the house, clean it out, bring water from the river, prepare food for him and also take care of the puppy's needs, thus making his life simpler. Incidentally, this assistant happens to be a woman. The disciple returns to his prescribed practices and his life carries on for a few months. After that his assistant starts telling him that they have need for money so that she can go to the city to buy the basic requirements and a few comforts for the house. So, now the disciple has to think of some way of making money to be able to keep his house in good shape and also to be able to pay the assistant and take care of the dog.

"He walks into the city one day to look for some part-time work, and finds a job working in a merchant's house helping him sort out his crop. He starts to work half the day with the merchant and the other half, he devotes to his own practices. This carries on for a few months and eventually comes a time when he realises that he is unable to do both at the same time.

"The dog by now has grown up, and one day returns with a female. Apparently, the female is pregnant, and is going to deliver puppies soon. His assistant comes to inform him that they must prepare for the birth of the puppies. She has even made a list of things they will require. The disciple comes to a point where he has to decide if he can give up his meditative practices to work a full-time job, and thereby earn enough money to be able to look after the assistant, the house and the family of dogs.

"He says to himself, 'I can't give up my responsibility towards all of them. After all, they were not in my life in the first place. It is I who brought them into my life. Later I can always go back to the practices that my master had instructed me to do. But, first, I must fulfil my responsibility at the present moment.' So, he gives up his practices completely and takes on a full-time job. He starts earning enough money to function the way he wants to. Eventually, he ends up marrying his assistant and starts his own family.

"Five years later, the master comes to the forest in search of his disciple. What he sees shocks him. Instead of seeing his disciple meditating and having grown spiritually in the direction his master wanted him to, he finds that he has become a family man. He has a large hut filled with the comforts of the world, a wife next to him, children running around, he is working full-time and also has a family of dogs which depend on him for sustenance.

"He goes up to his disciple and asks, 'What happened? How have you reached this stage?' That is the moment when the truth hits the disciple. He recalls all that has happened to him in the past five years. He tells the master the whole incident and says, 'I thought it was a test. I thought that the injured puppy was a test. And, because you had always told us that we must be compassionate and loving, and always give help to those in need, I could not go any other way. I had to help the puppy.'

"The master then tells him, 'It was indeed a test. But, it was a test of your understanding of my instructions, of your faithfulness to your master's words and orders. Just before you left for the forest, I had told you that the practices and the goal must be kept in front of you at all times. Get attached or carried away by nothing else. So, the injured dog was truly a test. But, it was a test of whether the goal was still in front of you. Your mission and task at that time was to be true to the words of your master. It was indeed a test. But, it was a test in which you failed, you did not succeed.'

"The disciple realises that instead of trying to fulfil his master's orders, which would make his life more simple and make it easier for him to follow the path and achieve his goal, a simple act like helping an injured puppy eventually led to his life becoming more and more complicated till there came a stage where he had to give up his primary goal and adopt a life which he never originally wanted, just because of the complications and responsibilities he had created around himself."

"What is the moral here, Suraj?" Nick asked.

"The moral is that one has to always keep one's main goal and purpose of life in front of oneself and not get involved in the many other smaller things which come before us and seem to be our duty also. If we get trapped in the small complications or problems of life and ignore our larger duty, we eventually tend to make the small traps into big webs that we cannot get out of," Suraj ended.

> *Keep in mind that any relationship is a physical experience that two spiritual beings are having!*

17

LIVING IN GOD

Nine and a half weeks were over and Suraj was leaving. We were at the airport and Suraj had already checked in for his flight back to India. I didn't know when I would see him next. I desperately sought some clarifications before he left.

"Suraj, over the past few weeks you have explained to me so much about different concepts, about different ways of looking at life, about the spiritual quest and about the growth of our soul. Now that you are leaving I am afraid I will become confused with all this knowledge, somewhat like the king you told me about. Please tell me a simple, easy way to follow and practise whatever it is you want me to do," I pleaded.

"It is good to see you ask for simplification again, Cathy," he said. "It doesn't matter what you do, if you do it in the smooth and simple way, you will arrive at your goal, faster and easier than the rest.'

"One of my friends in the Special Forces once told me that whenever they sit down to plan any important mission, they always keep a basic principle in mind. The principle he called the 'KISS' principle, and do you know what the letters stand for, Cathy? Keep It Simple, Soldier!

"This friend of mine said that no matter how complicated a plan gets initially, in the end they always evaluate it by putting it up against the KISS principle. They sit down with the plan that all their minds together have made up and evaluate it to see if it really is a simple plan, and if not, then now they can make it so. The secret of their success, they believe, is simplicity. If the plan is simple, it will work, and if it is not, it will not work because there will be too many complications arising once the plan is in operation. They believe that if you don't make your plan simple, you're stupid. So, I am glad that you ask me for more simplification, for it is truly the key to travelling fast and light to your goal.

"You remember, in our initial meetings I told you that there is a common thread running through all of us here, everything inanimate and animate, living and non-living? And that common factor in all of us, that common energy, is God.

"Now, your end goal is to recognise God as the common factor in each and everything in your life. Not only to know that He is there, Cathy, but to really live with that realisation all the time. As you go through your day, as you go through your life, you have to believe that everything that comes across you is full of God, whether it be people, incidents, or any other things, God is in all of them."

"I understand that," I interrupted.

"Also, you must believe God is in you. You cannot separate yourself from God and feel that God is in everything outside of you. You must believe that God is in everything outside and inside of you, and it is not just a simple intellectual knowing. It has to be experienced and you have to live in this realisation all the time. Now that is your goal."

"So what's the easiest way to do that?" I asked.

"What is the simple way to get there? Let me tell you more about that. You see, God gave you many tools. Your mind is a tool. The mind has certain offshoots—ambitions, desires, anger, pride. All of these things are good in their own way. But, when they are used for misjudged aims or goals, then they become bad. For example, anger, if used for a good and righteous purpose, is good anger, and if used for a bad and selfish purpose, is bad anger. And eventually, you use your mind itself as a springboard to reach that stage beyond the mind where you become one in God.

"But, try and understand that on a daily basis how can you start fighting with your own mind? Your mind is something you have been using for the last 30-40 years. As you grow up, your parents teach you that it is very important to have a good, calculative, analytical mind. The whole stress in today's society is on developing your mind because the world believes that your mind is the tool for success. So, all of a sudden when you have been using your mind? for 30-40 years, it is impossible to start fighting against it or start leaving it behind. It just does not happen. There are too many things that you have to fight against. Like I told you, selfishness, pride, anger, possessiveness, jealousy. All of these things come to you through your mind, and if you start fighting against your mind, you will be defeated—absolutely, certainly and fast. It is impossible to win. You can't.

"It is as if there are five or six enemies standing against you and you are alone. They are all attacking you at the same time. How can you even think of fighting against them and winning?" Suraj said.

"So how do I go about it then? What is the way to overcome the mind?"

"Cathy, what happens when you know that the forces arrayed against you are much stronger? You know you can't fight against them single-handed. What do you do then?

"The easiest way to face them is to go and find an ally. An ally who is much stronger than you, much bigger than you and one who is also much bigger than your enemies.

"Once you have that ally standing with you, then you can stand still and face your enemies, and tell them, 'Okay, come on, I am ready for you.' And they, seeing that you are standing along with your strong ally, will not come forward, they will back out.

"Now this ally that I want you to have in your life all the time is God. Keep God with you all the time. Develop a friendly relationship with Him. Be respectful of Him and more than anything else be in love with Him. Keep Him with you all the time and get lost in Him. He gave you your mind and He'll help you overcome it.

"Eventually, if you have a stronger ally, you have to start listening to what He says. You can't keep telling Him what to do all the time. If you want to continue to have Him on your side, you have to start listening. Don't you?

"So, start listening to God. Keep Him by your side all the time and you will realise that every time your mind starts to act upon you or your anger, pride and judgements come forward, if you remember God at that time, you will overcome these emotions of anger, pride, jealousy, judgements or whatever it is that's troubling you.

"That is the simple rule of overcoming your mind.

"Every time something starts to bother you, go to God."

"Every time you feel fear, go to God.

"Keep God with you all the time.

"That is the simple rule. Eventually one day you will realise that you have reached a stage where you have overcome or gone beyond your mind and you will start to see God in everything around you.

"Keeping God with you at every moment of life consciously is the simplest way of reaching the goal.

"Remember that there are no guarantees in this world, nothing is certain and nothing is fixed. Everything is changing all the time. The only one who is not changing, who is stable and who is available all the time for us is God. And the only place you'll eventually end up is back with Him.

"As you go through life, everything in and around you changes. People grow. Even your husband grows every day. Your friends grow, they change, they have their own lives to lead.

"You feel your children are yours and love you a lot. After fifteen years, they want to be independent. Your parents who have been taking care of you and who provide you with very stable support in life, will eventually die and you will be alone.

"But, the one throughout your life who remains unchanging is God.

"So, as you walk on this path, remember a small formula, which is, remember that God is always there to help you on your way. What He expects of you is only to trust Him and to pray, for He is the one and only true friend whom you can really depend on till the very end. So, use this friend to change your entire life. Just keep Him near you and take His support. Every time something comes in your life, go to Him, seek His help, seek His security, seek His support and get lost in Him. Let Him guide you through all your problems. He will never ever let you down. Do you follow?" Suraj asked.

"Yes," I replied hesitatingly.

"And, since I am leaving now, Cathy, I must leave you with a small humorous anecdote which goes like this.

"One day, in a small country town, there was a priest who had tremendous faith in God. He would spend his whole day absorbed in the thought of God and knew that God took care of everything and everybody all the time.

"Once it happened that the town he lived in was flooded and all the houses were washed away in the flood. Lots of people were dying everywhere. There were rescue operations being conducted by the Government, and helicopters were being sent to airlift the people out of trouble.

"Since it was a small town, most people frequently went to church and everybody knew the priest. They all had respect for his faith in God. So, imagine the scene, there is water everywhere and this priest is hanging on to a broken tree, which is floating in all this water, and along with him on the same tree are a lady and three of her children.

"The priest is praying to God even while hanging on to the tree trunk and he is saying, 'God, I know You will help me, I have full faith in You, I have lived my life for You, I have spoken Your word and I have encouraged the people to seek support in You. I know You will not let me down. You have sent this flood and You will save me from it.'

"What happens next is that one of the soldiers in a rescue boat sees the priest, the woman and her three children hanging on to the tree, and he brings his boat towards them. When he comes near, he puts his hand out and says, 'Priest, come with me, I'll save you.'

"The priest, because he sees the woman and the children there and wonders what hey will think of him says, 'No, no, no, please take the children first. I will be okay. God will take care of me.'

"The soldier says, 'No priest, you come first, I will take care of them later.'

"The priest replies, 'No, I am fine. I told you, God will take care of me. He is not going to let me die. Please take the children first.'

"So, the soldier reluctantly takes the children to safety. He comes back and says to the priest, 'Come with me quickly. The water is rising, I will save you.'

"Again the priest tells him, 'No, please take the woman before me. You have to save her. You have saved her children. They will need their mother. You can come back for me later. I know nothing is going to happen to me. God is going to save me.'

"The soldier again tells him, 'Come, priest; the water is rising. Come with me now, I'll save you. I'll come back for the woman if I can.'

"The priest again tells him, 'No, please take the woman first.'

"So, the soldier reluctantly takes the woman away to safety, and before he can come back for the priest, the water rises and the priest drowns."

"The priest drowns?" I asked.

"Yes, when the priest goes to heaven, he can't believe that God allowed him to drown and didn't come for his help. He approaches God and tells Him, 'You know, God, I spent my whole life talking about You, thinking about You. In Your service, I guided others about you. I did whatever You commanded me to do. I had full faith in You. You knew what was happening to me and You still didn't come down to save me. I repeatedly requested You to save me. And You still didn't come. Why?'

"God listens quietly to the priest till he stops talking. God then smiles and tells the priest, 'My son, I always hear you. And even this instance I heard you the very first time you asked for My help. I came twice to help you on the boat and both times you sent Me away.'

"Cathy, this was where the priest lacked in faith. If we keep God as our ally all the time, spend our life with Him and have faith in Him, then we must also have faith that whatever happens is happening for our own good through the same God that we have asked for help. When the boat came to save the priest, instead of accepting it as God's will that he be saved first, his own pride and self-righteousness came in the way. He said, 'No, save the children first,' because he thought that if he went first, what would the lady and the children think of him.

"If he had full faith, he would have accepted the fact that the soldier who came to his help and asked him to come on to the boat also came by God's will and he would have been saved. But, because he got lost in his own pride and ego, he lacked in faith, and that is why he had to face the results of his own consequences.

"Now, Cathy, time to be on my way. I shall seek you out again soon, though I do not know exactly when that will be," Suraj said.

"I will be waiting for you whenever you decide to come back, Suraj. And, please keep in touch with me over the phone. You know, I will need your help a lot in trying to follow this path that you have asked me to walk."

"I'll always be there for you, Cathy. Whenever the need is true, I will always be available. Not only me, but all the masters who have walked this path before us and God Himself will guide and empower you, Don't worry about that. In the meantime, though, I have one request of you."

"Whatever you say, Suraj, whatever you ask me to do," I replied eagerly.

"What I want you to do, Cathy, is to wait for a couple of days after I have returned, and then to sit down and write about what the last nine and a half weeks have been for you. Try and recall not only from your mind, but also from your heart. Try and recollect all that you can about whatever we have spoken and what you have understood."

"But, it will be impossible for me to write what you spoke without my own understanding blended into it," I said.

"In fact, I want you to use your own understanding to write, using both your mind and your heart. This is critical. So, remember this, not only your mind, you must recall also with your heart. Then, write down whatever has happened between us in the last nine and a half weeks. Can you do that?" Suraj asked.

"I'll try my best," I answered.

"That's all you need to do, Cathy. If you keep God by your side in whatever you do in life, all you really need to do is sincerely try your best and then He will take care of the rest. But it must be sincerely your best. Remember this also, another good formula to keep with you," he smiled. "And, when it's complete, don't forget to send me a copy."

And with that he turned and hugged me! A full, frontal body hug—and what a hug! I felt completely surrounded by love—so protected, so comfortable, so free. I melted and my tears started to flow.

I couldn't stop. I didn't want to stop. They were tears of happiness, of gratitude. We remained hugging for a few minutes and then we parted.

Suraj walked into the immigration and security area of the airport. I waited outside for some time and then got into my car and returned home.

Since then, I spent a number of days thinking about what happened, feeling what happened between us. Eventually I sat down and started writing.

Nick helped me along the way. It was amazing how our relationship had become enriched in Suraj's company. We had become closer to each other than ever before.

I mailed him a copy when I finished.

About a month later, I received a card from him which had the words, **"Welcome to the club, Cathy. You are a full-time member now"**, written on the front page.

I have wondered many times since then which club he was referring to. I must remember to ask him about it the next time we meet.

I turned the page over. Inside the card were the words **"Remember your lessons well. Help yourself first and then God shall help you to help others.**

> *Yours,*
> *Suraj"*

> *True surrender means*
> *putting God's will before*
> *your own!*

AFTERWORD

My purpose in writing this book was to make the universal spiritual laws of awareness and purpose available to a wide readership in the simplest language possible. My intention was to make difficult cosmic principles easy to understand and to practise in our daily lives.

I believe that relationships are extremely important in our spiritual growth. As you look around you, you will notice that all kinds of relationships are at a stage in this world's evolution where maximum turbulence and disharmony is created in them. The main reason for disharmonious relationships are the people involved in them. In this book, I have tried to explain how two people can accept each other and thereby make their relationship one which allows each one to grow spiritually, and at the same time, to give love to the other openly and fully with a spiritual motive.

Children are also very close to my heart and I am deeply touched by the fact that troubled and disharmonious relationships affect children even more than the adults involved in them. So in this book, it has been my sincere effort to try to create awareness in the readers of the true spiritual purpose of any relationship. Or any kind of interaction between human beings.

As we go through our lives, I believe that the teachings of the spiritual masters and the ancient scriptures should not only be in our minds, but should also be applied in our daily lives. I believe that it is in the living out of these principles that one can grow spiritually and become more complete.

As I said in the introduction, this book has been growing inside me for a long time and eventually when I started to act on this inner inspiration, I always kept a goal in front of me. My goal was to keep these teachings simple and concise, to be able to give the readers a comfortable way to incorporate them into daily life and relationships. Happiness is not a mere concept which should only be discussed and debated, but a true value which should be apparent in our lives and must pervade our interactions with people.

We are all children of God and He has created this world as an ideal classroom for our spiritual growth. One of the central messages of this book is that we should accept everyone and everything around us as a means and a guide towards our greater self. We must learn to use everything that we come across to raise our consciousness and become closer to the ultimate reality.

In the course of my counselling, people have often told me how my my words have helped and comforted them. If this book has touched you in any way, or helped you through any crisis, please write to me at the following address:

Vikas Malkani,
C-36, Mayfair Gardens,
New Delhi-110016. (India)

I shall sincerely try and include some of the letters in my forthcoming book.